OCCASIONAL PAPER **196**

Trade and Trade Policies in Eastern and Southern Africa

By a staff team led by Arvind Subramanian

**With Enrique Gelbard, Richard Harmsen,
Katrin Elborgh-Woytek, and Piroska Nagy**

INTERNATIONAL MONETARY FUND
Washington DC
August, 2000

Production: IMF Graphics Section
Charts: Sana Elaroussi
Typesetting: Alicia Etchebarne-Bourdin

Library of Congress Cataloging-in-Publication Data

Trade and trade policies in eastern and southern Africa/prepared by a staff
team led by Arvind Subramanian; with Enrique Gelbard . . . [et al.].

p.   cm. — (IMF occasional paper ; 196)

ISBN 1-55775-942-1

Includes bibliographical references.

1. Africa, Eastern—Commerce. 2. Africa, Southern—Commerce. 3.
Africa, Eastern—Foreign economic relations. 4. Africa, Southern—Foreign
economic relations. I. Subramanian, Arvind. II. Series. III. Occasional
Paper (International Monetary Fund); no. 196.

HF3892.Z5T73 2000
382'.09676—dc21   00-063446
                                                             CIP

Price: US$20.00
(US$17.50 to full-time faculty members and
students at universities and colleges)

Please send orders to:
International Monetary Fund, Publication Services
700 19th Street, N.W., Washington, D.C. 20431, U.S.A.
Tel.: (202) 623-7430   Telefax: (202) 623-7201
E-mail: publications@imf.org
Internet: http://www.imf.org

recycled paper

Contents

The following symbols have been used throughout this paper:

. . . to indicate that data are not available;

— to indicate that the figure is zero or less than half the final digit shown, or that the item does not exist;

– between years or months (e.g., 1998–99 or January–June) to indicate the years or months covered, including the beginning and ending years or months;

/ between years (e.g., 1998/99) to indicate a fiscal (financial) year.

"Billion" means a thousand million.

Minor discrepancies between constituent figures and totals are due to rounding.

The term "country," as used in this paper, does not in all cases refer to a territorial entity that is a state as understood by international law and practice; the term also covers some territorial entities that are not states, but for which statistical data are maintained and provided internationally on a separate and independent basis.

List of Abbreviations

BLNS	Botswana, Lesotho, Namibia, and Swaziland
CBI	Cross-Border Initiative
COMESA	Common Market for Eastern and Southern Africa
DRC	Democratic Republic of Congo
EAC	Commission for East African Cooperation
EPZ	export processing zone
ESA	Eastern and Southern Africa
EU	European Union
EU-SA FTA	EU-South Africa free trade agreement
FTA	free trade agreement
IOC	Indian Ocean Commission
ITU	International Telecommunications Union
MERCOSUR	Common Market of the South
MFN	most-favored nation
NAFTA	North American Free Trade Agreement
NGO	Nongovernment organization
NTB	nontariff barrier
ODC	Other duties and charges
RTA	regional trade arrangement
SACU	Southern African Customs Union
SADC	Southern African Development Community
SSA	sub-Saharan Africa
SITC	Standard International Trade Classification
TFP	total factor productivity
WAEMU	West African Economic and Monetary Union
WTO	World Trade Organization

Preface

This occasional paper analyzes trade and trade policy developments in the countries of eastern and southern Africa during the 1990s, covering regional and multilateral integration issues, and the interaction between trade policies and macroeconomic conditions. It also discusses the main challenges these countries face as they enter a new decade.

The authors are indebted to Anupam Basu for his guidance and support to carry out this work. Jon Shields, Joseph Kakoza, Mwanza Nkusu, Gunnar Jonsson, Berte Esteve-Volart, Anne McGuirk, and John King provided valuable input to the paper. The paper has also benefited from comments by the Fiscal Affairs, Policy Development and Review, and Research Departments of the IMF. The research assistance of Jaouad Sebti, the editorial assistance of Thomas Walter and Jeremy Clift, and the secretarial support of Mariza Arantes are gratefully acknowledged.

The views expressed here are those of the authors and do not necessarily reflect the opinions of other members of the IMF staff or its Executive Directors.

I Overview

Since the early 1990s, many countries in sub-Saharan Africa have made significant progress in opening their economies to external competition through trade and exchange liberalization, often in the context of IMF and World Bank-supported programs. African liberalization took place during a period of increasing globalization of trade and investment, the conclusion of the Uruguay Round of trade negotiations, and the creation or expansion of a number of important regional trade arrangements in other parts of the world. These initiatives contributed to a revival of interest among African policymakers in regional integration, resulting in the establishment or renewal of regional organizations, such as the West African Economic and Monetary Union (WAEMU), the Cross-Border Initiative (CBI), the Southern African Development Community (SADC), the Common Market for Eastern and Southern Africa (COMESA), the Commission for East African Cooperation (EAC), and the Indian Ocean Commission (IOC) (Table 1.1).

This paper analyzes trade and trade policy developments for a number of countries in the eastern and southern African region (referred to here as ESA) during the 1990s.[1] It consists of three main parts: a descriptive one (Sections II-V), an analytical one (Section VI), and a normative one (Section VII). Section II provides a brief description of the region, while Sections III and IV elaborate on the domestic liberalization efforts of these countries: the former focuses on nonpreferential liberalization and the latter focuses on preferential/regional liberalization. Section V deals with the external trade policy environment facing ESA countries and the changes in openness and export performance witnessed in recent years. Drawing from the experience of individual countries in the region, Section VI contains an analysis of the macroeconomic aspects of trade re-

forms, including the factors that have influenced trade liberalization efforts and the impact of these reforms on economic growth. Finally, Section VII addresses the main trade policy issues that these countries will face in the future and suggests possible actions they and their trading partners could follow.

Why focus on eastern and southern Africa? The answer is twofold. First, countries in ESA appear to have a number of common characteristics—most notably administrative and legal institutions and language—stemming in part from a shared colonial history. Second, an increasing number of ESA countries are coming together—in various configurations and at varying speeds—to forge stronger trading links among themselves. Thus, the region as a whole is becoming a natural unit of analysis from a trade perspective.

The following conclusions emerge from the study. First, a number of countries in ESA made significant progress toward opening up their economies during the 1990s. Between 1990 and 1998, low levels of trade restrictiveness (covering both trade taxes and nontariff trade barriers) were established in 10 of the 22 countries considered. The remaining countries, however, still maintain restrictive or moderately restrictive trade regimes. Trade reforms aimed at, and broadly achieved, a substantial reduction in nontariff barriers, import tariffs, and export taxes, alongside complementary liberalization measures in other areas, including the relaxation of foreign exchange controls. As a result, many countries narrowed, but still did not eliminate, the gap in terms of trade restrictiveness between their regimes and those of other regions of the world.

Second, in the area of services, notably in the banking and telecommunications sectors, ESA countries have more restrictive regimes than other countries. Moreover, in the area of trade in goods and services, they have not really used the World Trade Organization (WTO) to further their liberalization efforts or lock in their current reforms, thereby forgoing some of the benefits that arise from ensuring against future policy reversals.

Third, there was an improvement in the trade performance of ESA countries during the 1990s, owing in part to the trade liberalization measures

---

[1]Throughout this paper, the ESA region will comprise the following 22 countries: Angola, Botswana, Burundi, Comoros, Democratic Republic of Congo, Eritrea, Ethiopia, Kenya, Lesotho, Madagascar, Malawi, Mauritius, Mozambique, Namibia, Rwanda, Seychelles, South Africa, Swaziland, Tanzania, Uganda, Zambia, and Zimbabwe.

Table 1.1. Selected African Countries' Membership in Regional Trade Agreements

	SADC	COMESA	SACU	CBI	EAC	IOC	WAEMU
Angola	✓	✓					
Benin							✓
Botswana	✓		✓				
Burkina Faso							✓
Burundi		✓		✓			
Comoros		✓		✓		✓	
Congo, Dem. Rep. of	✓	✓					
Côte d'Ivoire							✓
Djibouti		✓					
Egypt		✓					
Eritrea		✓					
Ethiopia		✓					
Guinea Bissau							✓
Kenya		✓		✓	✓		
Lesotho	✓		✓				
Madagascar		✓		✓		✓	
Malawi	✓	✓		✓			
Mali							✓
Mauritius	✓	✓		✓		✓	
Mozambique	✓						
Namibia	✓	✓	✓	✓			
Niger							✓
Rwanda		✓		✓			
Senegal							✓
Seychelles	✓	✓		✓		✓	
South Africa	✓		✓				
Sudan		✓					
Swaziland	✓	✓	✓	✓			
Tanzania	✓	✓		✓	✓		
Togo							✓
Uganda		✓		✓	✓		
Zambia	✓	✓		✓			
Zimbabwe	✓	✓		✓			

Notes: SADC = Southern African Development Community; COMESA = Common Market for Eastern and Southern Africa; SACU = Southern African Customs Union; CBI = Cross-Border Initiative; EAC = Commission for East African Cooperation; IOC = Indian Ocean Commission; WAEMU = West African Economic and Monetary Union.

adopted. Exports, in particular manufactured exports, posted gains during the 1990s. This trend was accompanied by only a modest increase in the diversity of exports. Thus, substantial progress is still required to increase the range and sophistication of products exported, as reflected in ESA's low share of intraindustry trade.

Fourth, links within the region are intensifying, as evidenced both by the magnitude of intraregional trade and the policy initiatives taken to reduce intraregional trade barriers. Progress in implementing these initiatives, however, remains mixed.

Fifth, adverse initial macroeconomic conditions in many ESA countries did not appear to hamper their trade liberalization efforts. Trade liberalization was associated with faster economic growth, especially when accompanied by comprehensive macroeconomic reforms. Trade liberalization also led to a significant reduction in the reliance on trade taxes as a source of revenue without compromising overall fiscal performance, owing to concomitant reforms to the tax system.

Sixth, a number of policy issues will confront ESA countries in the years ahead, especially in light of the likely changes in their trading environment:

• There is a considerable unfinished agenda on trade liberalization, especially for the nine countries that continue to maintain restrictive trade regimes.

- In proceeding with preferential integration, ESA countries need to rationalize the multiplicity of regional initiatives and pursue simultaneous multilateral liberalization in order to maximize the potential benefits of globalization and mitigate the trade diversion effects of their regional integration schemes.

- In the future, ESA countries will need to reassess their role in the WTO, with a view to increasing the benefits that they can derive from it. For instance, they could use the WTO as an anchor to lock in their liberalization of trade in goods and services. ESA countries will also need to respond to reductions in their trade-related revenues and in preferential access to industrial country markets. These are likely to arise as a result of future regional and multilateral liberalization initiatives.

- Lastly, industrial countries could help facilitate ESA countries' integration into the world economy by either entering into reciprocal free trade agreements with ESA countries or eliminating tariffs on ESA's export products. Industrial countries could also forgo the right to use safeguards or antidumping actions against these exports.

II Eastern and Southern Africa: Broad Characteristics of the Region

The 22 eastern and southern African countries covered in this study vary considerably in population, size, and economic profile (Table 2.1). Population size varies from fewer than 80,000 people in Seychelles to about 62 million people in Ethiopia. The average per capita income of about US$1,100 also masks large variations across countries. The Seychelles is the richest country, with a per capita GDP of about US$6,000 at 1990 prices, while the Democratic Republic of Congo (DRC) stands as the poorest country, with an income per capita of US$99 (a ratio of 60 to 1). There is also a wide variation in income inequality among countries. For example, the Gini coefficient, which measures income inequality,

Table 2.1. Eastern and Southern Africa: Basic Economic Indicators

| | Population[1] (Millions) | Area[2] (000 sq. km.) | GDP per Capita[3] (US$) | GDP[4] (US$ billion) | Growth of GDP per Capita[5] | | | Gini Coefficient[6] |
					1980–89	1990–94	1995–99	
Angola	12.8	1,247	830	6.4	–1.1	–8.0	3.5	...
Botswana	1.6	567	3,640	5.2	7.3	2.0	2.7	...
Burundi	6.2	26	163	1.0	0.7	–1.5	–2.8	...
Comoros	0.6	2	438	0.2	0.0	–0.4	–3.1	...
Congo, Dem. Rep. of	45.9	2,267	99	3.0	–1.0	–11.2	–6.6	...
Eritrea	...	101	...	0.6	...	...	...	...
Ethiopia	61.7	1,000	193	6.7	–0.9	0.3	4.8	40
Kenya	30.0	569	342	10.6	0.9	–3.4	0.3	45
Lesotho	2.2	2	401	0.9	1.9	1.4	2.1	56
Madagascar	15.0	582	233	3.7	–2.1	–3.1	0.0	46
Malawi	11.0	94	226	1.8	–1.4	–2.0	5.2	...
Mauritius	1.2	2	3,151	4.0	3.8	4.2	3.7	...
Mozambique	17.3	784	249	4.1	–0.7	0.7	6.0	...
Namibia	1.8	823	1,810	3.0	–2.4	0.7	–0.5	...
Rwanda	7.1	25	342	2.0	–1.4	–12.1	11.4	29
Seychelles	0.1	0.5	5,999	0.6	1.8	3.1	1.1	...
South Africa	43.2	1,221	2,943	131.0	–0.2	–2.5	–0.3	59
Swaziland	...	17	1,091	1.2	2.0	0.6	1.0	...
Tanzania	32.6	884	189	8.6	–0.6	–0.2	1.6	38
Uganda	22.2	200	327	5.8	–0.3	1.8	4.8	39
Zambia	10.0	743	351	3.1	–1.7	–2.9	–0.5	50
Zimbabwe	13.1	387	805	5.7	1.6	–0.9	–0.1	57

[1]IMF: *World Economic Outlook* database, 2000.
[2]World Bank data.
[3]1999 real per capita GDP (U.S. dollars at 1990 prices and 1990 exchange rates).
[4]1999 gross domestic product (in U.S. dollars at current prices).
[5]Annual average real per capita GDP growth (in percent).
[6]Gini index from Table 2.8 of World Bank, *World Development Indicators*, 1999.

varies from 29 in Rwanda to 59 in South Africa, the latter being among the highest in the world.

Many countries in the ESA region experienced an improvement in economic performance in the second half of the 1990s, with 13 of 22 countries exhibiting increases in per capita GDP. South Africa dominates the economic landscape of the region, accounting for 62 percent of ESA's GDP and 74 percent of its exports. It is also dominant in terms of the industrial base, the amount of skilled manpower, the quality of its physical and financial infrastructure, and the maturity of domestic institutions and of the legal and regulatory frameworks.

Agriculture accounts for a large (about 26 percent) albeit declining share of output in ESA countries (see Appendix II, Table A1). ESA countries are more dependent than middle-income countries on agriculture, although the disparity between the two groups is less if shares are computed on a weighted-average basis

because of the relatively small share of agriculture in South Africa.[2] Angola is the only fuel-based economy.

There is a corresponding disparity in the industrial sector, as ESA countries generate less than 30 percent of output (35 percent on a weighted average basis) in that sector, compared with 42 percent in middle-income countries. The Southern African Customs Union (SACU) countries (Botswana, Lesotho, Namibia, South Africa, and Swaziland), Zambia, and Mauritius are the most manufacturing-intensive economies in the region.

Services account for roughly the same share of output in both ESA and middle-income countries. The island economies (Comoros, Madagascar, Mauritius, and Seychelles), Botswana, Kenya, Namibia, South Africa, Zambia, and Zimbabwe derive more than 50 percent of their output from services.

---

[2]Middle-income countries are defined by the World Bank as those with a 1998 per capita GNP of between US$760 and US$9,360.

III Trade Liberalization by ESA Countries During the 1990s

Unilateral Liberalization in Goods

In the early 1990s, reflecting the inward-looking development policies adopted in previous decades, the trade and exchange regimes of most countries in eastern and southern Africa were characterized by multiple exchange rate systems, surrender requirements for export proceeds, high tariff protection, restrictive import licensing requirements, and other restrictive nontariff barriers. The restrictiveness of the trade regimes during the 1990s is depicted in Tables 3.1 to 3.3, which classify the trade systems based on a scheme that captures both tariff and nontariff barriers.[3] As shown in Table 3.1, at the beginning of the decade, the average indicator of trade restrictiveness for the region as a whole was 9.7 (on a scale from 0 to 10, where 10 indicates the most restrictive regime). Table 3.2 shows that 16 of the 22 ESA countries had highly restrictive nontariff barriers in place, while the remaining 6 had substantial restrictions as well. Total trade taxes (including import tariffs, export levies, and other duties and charges) averaged 38 percent (Table 3.3), and tariff dispersion was quite high.[4] The transparency of the tariff regime was hampered by the large number of tariff bands and by frequent changes in the classification of products. In this regard, SACU's tariff regime offered an extreme example: the product classification was changed on a weekly or even a daily basis, thereby contributing to the high degree of unpredictability of the regime. Furthermore, governments usually tried to reduce the anti-export bias of high trade protection by granting discretionary exemptions on inputs and capital goods, thereby reducing the transparency of the trade regime and increasing opportunities for abuse and corruption.

Changes During the 1990s

Many countries liberalized their trade regime during the 1990s and introduced economic reform programs to reduce the role of the state in the economy and enhance private sector growth. Policy measures included price liberalization, deregulation, and privatization of state enterprises, often in the context of IMF-supported programs[5] (Box 3.1) and with the support of the CBI. These policy changes reflected the recognition that reliance on administrative controls had driven much economic activity outside formal channels, depressed exports, contributed to an inefficient structure of domestic production, and hampered long-run growth. In addition, the improvement in foreign relations in the southern African region, following the demise of the apartheid regime in South Africa, strongly reduced the political motives for inward-looking economic policies. Although the nature, extent, and timing of trade liberalization in ESA countries during the 1990s differed,[6] many countries made substantial progress in opening their economies during this period.

As a result of these efforts, ESA countries' trade regimes are converging toward those of the rest of the world.[7] Nevertheless, the overall restrictiveness of trade regimes in eastern and southern Africa remains higher than that of all other groups of countries in the world (Table 3.4), and not all the coun-

---

[3]The trade restrictiveness index is a modified version of the one used in Sharer and others (1998), and is based on a classification system for nontariff barriers and for import and export taxes (see Appendix I).

[4]For example, in the case of South Africa and its partners in SACU, the maximum tariff was 1,389 percent, there were more than 13,000 tariff lines, and the effective protection ranged from −411 to 189 percent. While extreme, South Africa's case was not atypical, as Malawi, Mauritius, and Ethiopia also had highly distorted tariff structures.

[5]Of the 22 countries in the ESA region, 14 had programs with the IMF during the 1990s. The SACU countries (excluding Lesotho), Angola, Eritrea, Mauritius, and the Seychelles did not have programs with the Fund (see Appendix II, Table A2).

[6]While some countries—Zambia, for example—embarked on a liberalization program that encompassed both tariff and nontariff barriers, some of the other reformers, such as Tanzania, gave priority to the elimination of nontariff barriers and reduced tariffs at a later stage.

[7]Tentative evidence derived from developments in tariff collection ratios and a categorization of countries on the basis of the Sachs-Warner criterion suggest that the gap between ESA countries and the rest of the world has narrowed considerably since the late 1980s (Appendix II, Table A3).

Table 3.1. Eastern and Southern Africa: Overall Trade Restrictiveness in the 1990s

	Initial Year	Index[1]	Final Year (end of period)	Index[1]	Change in Index	Reversal[2]
Countries with restrictive regimes in 1998						
Angola	1991	10	1998	10	0	Yes
Burundi	1991	10	1998	10	0	Yes
Comoros	1990	10	1998	10	0	Yes
Ethiopia	1992	10	1998	8	−2	No
Eritrea	1990	10	1998	10	0	No
Kenya	1990	10	1998	7	−3	No
Mauritius	1991	10	1998	7	−3	No
Seychelles	1991	10	1998	10	0	Yes
Zimbabwe	1992	10	1998	9	−1	Yes
Average		10.0		9.0	−1.0	
Countries with moderately restrictive regimes in 1998						
Madagascar	1991	10	1998	5	−5	No
Rwanda	1993	10	1998	5	−5	No
Tanzania[3]	1990	10	1998	6	−4	Yes
Average		10.0		5.3	−4.7	
Countries with moderately open regimes in 1998						
Botswana	1990	10	1998	4	−6	No
Congo, Dem. Rep. of	1993	9	1997	4	−5	No
Lesotho	1990	10	1998	4	−6	No
Malawi[3]	1992	7	1998	4	−3	Yes
Namibia	1990	10	1998	4	−6	No
South Africa	1990	10	1998	4	−6	No
Swaziland	1990	10	1998	4	−6	No
Average		9.4		4.0	−5.4	
Countries with open regimes in 1998						
Mozambique	1991	7	1998	2	−5	No
Uganda	1991	10	1998	1	−9	No
Zambia	1991	10	1998	2	−8	Yes
Average		9.0		1.7	−7.3	
Average for all ESA countries		9.7		5.9	−3.8	

Source: IMF staff estimates.

[1]This index is based upon the classification scheme developed by Sharer and others (1998) but differs from it in two main respects. First, export tariffs are explicitly taken into account. Second, wherever a country's trade taxes exceed 35 percent, it is accorded a 10 rating irrespective of its regime for nontariff barriers (Appendix I). A rating of between 7 and 10 classifies a country as restrictive; 5 or 6 as "moderately restrictive"; 3 or 4 as "moderately open"; and 1 or 2 as "open."

[2]A reversal is said to have occurred when trade taxes have increased or quantitative restrictions intensified during 1991–98.

[3]Further trade liberalization measures were undertaken in 1999.

tries in the region have participated in the general trend toward opening their economies. One set of countries achieved relatively little or no liberalization (such as Angola, Burundi, Comoros, and Zimbabwe) and, hence, remained quite closed, while another achieved substantial liberalization, including, among others, Mozambique, Malawi, Uganda, the countries in the SACU, and Zambia.

Trade reforms were characterized by the following elements:

- *The reduction or elimination of nontariff barriers.* This comprised the elimination of import and export quotas, bans, state trading, and other nontariff barriers. As of end-1998, five countries in the region (the Democratic Republic of Congo, Mozambique, Rwanda, Uganda, and Zambia) had eliminated all nontariff barriers that were in place at the beginning of the decade—with the exception of restrictions related to health, environmental, and security reasons—

Table 3.2. Eastern and Southern Africa: Measure of Trade Restrictiveness in the 1990s: Nontariff Barrier (NTB) Regimes

	Initial Year	Categorization	Final Year	Restrictions	Observations on Current Situation
Countries with pervasive NTB regimes at end–1998					
Angola	1991	Pervasive	1998	Pervasive	All imports subject to foreign exchange restrictions; restrictive licensing of exports and imports.
Burundi	1991	Pervasive	1998	Pervasive	Imports subject to exchange restrictions and suspension of provision of foreign exchange for luxury products. State trading in the coffee sector.
Seychelles	1990	Pervasive	1998	Pervasive	Commercial imports subject to quota. Import monopoly for a large number of consumer goods.
Countries with substantial NTB restrictions at end–1998					
Eritrea	1990	Pervasive	1998	Substantial	Export and import bans for a few items. State trading in tobacco and matches.
Ethiopia	1992	Pervasive	1998	Substantial	State trading in petroleum and import licensing.
Kenya	1990	Pervasive	1998	Substantial	Restrictions on exports of tea, coffee, minerals, and agricultural products.
Mauritius	1991	Substantial	1998	Substantial	Government monopoly on oil and cement imports; state trading.
Zimbabwe	1992	Pervasive	1998	Substantial	Restrictions on exports of maize, wheat, and minerals.
Countries with few NTB restrictions at end–1998					
Botswana	1991	Pervasive	1998	Few	Follows in general South Africa's import regime.
Comoros	1990	Pervasive	1998	Few	No restrictive licensing for imports. Government monopoly on oil imports.
Lesotho	1992	Pervasive	1998	Few	Follows in general South Africa's import regime.
Namibia	1992	Pervasive	1998	Few	Follows in general South Africa's import regime.
Madagascar	1991	Substantial	1998	Few	Government monopoly on oil imports; eliminated in 1999.
Malawi	1992	Substantial	1998	Few	Restrictive licensing requirement for fuel (including petroleum).
Tanzania	1990	Pervasive	1998	Few	Government monopoly on oil imports; eliminated in 1999.
Swaziland	1992	Pervasive	1998	Few	Follows in general South Africa's import regime.
South Africa	1992	Pervasive	1998	Few	Active antidumping policy.
Countries with no NTB restrictions at end–1998					
Congo, Dem. Rep. of	1993	Substantial	1997	None	No NTBs, except for health and security reasons.
Uganda	1991	Substantial	1998	None	Import ban on cigarettes; removed in 1999.
Mozambique	1993	Substantial	1998	None	No NTBs, except for health and security reasons.
Rwanda	1993	Pervasive	1998	None	No NTBs, except for health, environmental, and security reasons.
Zambia	1991	Pervasive	1998	None	No NTBs, except for health, environmental, and security reasons.

Source: IMF staff estimates.

Table 3.3. Eastern and Southern Africa: Trade Tax Regimes in the 1990s

	Initial Year	Average Import Tariff[1]	Average Export Tariff[2]	Total[3]	Final Year (end of period)	Average Import Tariff[1]	Average Export Tariff[2]	Total[3]	Change in Import Tariff[1]	Change in Export Tariff[1]	Change in Trade Taxes[1]
Countries with trade taxes greater than 25 percent in 1998											
Burundi	1991	39	2	41	1998	41	24	75	2	23	34
Comoros	1991	62	3	67[4]	1998	71	2	74[4]	9	-1	8
Eritrea	1993	...	21	...	1998	60	0	60	...	-21	...
Rwanda	1993	35	18	59[5]	1998	22	5	28[5]	-13	-13	-31
Seychelles	1991	85	0	85[4]	1998	38	0	38[4]	-47	0	-47
Zimbabwe	1992	30	0	30	1998	32	0	32	2	0	2
Average		50	7	56		44	5	51	-6	-2	-5
Countries with trade taxes between 15 percent and 25 percent in 1998											
Angola	1991	24	...	24	1998	24	0	24	0	...	0
Congo, Dem. Rep. of	1993	20	8	30[7]	1997	17	5	23[5]	-3	-3	-7
Ethiopia	1992	79	4	86	1998	17	4	21	-62	0	-64
Kenya	1990	44	0	44	1998	19	0	19[6]	-25	0	-25
Madagascar	1991	30	8	40	1998	18	0	18	-12	-8	-22
Mauritius	1991	34	10	46	1998	19	0	19[7]	-15	-10	-27
Tanzania	1990	25	0	25[5]	1998	20	0	20[5]	-5	0	-5
Average		36	5	42		19	1	21	-17	-4	-21
Countries with trade taxes less than 15 percent in 1998											
Botswana	1990	45	0	45	1998	15	0	15	-30	0	-30
Lesotho	1990	45	0	45	1998	15	0	15	-30	0	-30
Malawi	1993	18	0	18	1998	12	0	12	-6	0	-6
Mozambique	1993	19	...	19	1998	10	-1	11[8]	-9	...	-6
Namibia	1990	45	0	45	1998	15	0	15	-30	0	-30
South Africa	1990	45	-1	45	1998	15	0	15	-30	0	-30
Swaziland	1990	45	0	45	1998	15	-1	15	-30	1	-29
Uganda	1991	18	13	33	1998	9	0	9	-9	-13	-24
Zambia	1991	37	0	37	1998	14	0	14	-23	0	-23
Average		35	2	37		13	0	13	-22	-1	-23
Overall average		35	3	38		15	1	15	-21	-2	-23

Source: IMF staff estimates.

[1]Statutory average tariff, including other duties and charges, unless indicated otherwise.

[2]Export tax revenue in percent of total exports.

[3]Based on the Lerner symmetry theorem, the total trade tax is defined as $[(1+m)*(1+x)-1]*100$ where m and x are the import and export tariff rates, respectively. Although the export tax is based on collections, there tends to be less divergence between statutory and collection rates on the export side than on the import side.

[4]The estimate is based on import tax revenue in percent of total imports and an assumed tax collection efficiency ratio of 50 percent.

[5]Trade-weighted average of import tariffs, including other duties and charges.

[6]The statutory average rate (including other duties and charges) is estimated at 19 percent, based on a collection rate of 12.5 percent.

[7]Estimate.

[8]Export tax revenue is estimated on the basis of the statutory tariff on exports of raw cashews (14 percent).

Box 3.1. Trade Liberalization in the Context of IMF-Supported Programs

During the 1990s, trade was liberalized in several ESA countries, including the fastest reformers (Mozambique, Uganda, and Zambia), under IMF and World Bank-supported programs.[1] In the case of Mozambique and Uganda, IMF programs were in place during the entire period under review. In addition, in several countries trade liberalization was pursued in the context of the Cross-Border Initiative

_____

[1]Programs lasted an average of 6.4 years and were, in six cases, nonconsecutive. With the exception of Lesotho (Stand-By, in addition to Structural Adjustment Facility (SAF)/Enhanced Structural Adjustment Facility (ESAF)), Zambia (Rights Accumulation Program, in addition to ESAF), and Zimbabwe (Extended Fund Facility and Stand-By arrangements, in addition to ESAF), all ESA countries using IMF resources were supported by SAF/ESAF arrangements.

(CBI), established with the support of the IMF, the World Bank, the EU, and the African Development Bank. Countries that changed from a restrictive regime in the early 1990s to a moderately restrictive regime in 1998 in the context of IMF-supported programs included the Democratic Republic of Congo, Malawi, Rwanda, and Tanzania.

Although Lesotho implemented programs supported by the IMF during the period 1990–97, as a member of SACU the country did not pursue an independent trade policy. Despite IMF-supported programs, Burundi, Comoros, Ethiopia, Kenya, Madagascar, and Zimbabwe ultimately achieved little or no liberalization in their trade regimes during the 1990s. The other countries with (relatively) restrictive regimes (Angola, Eritrea, Mauritius, and Seychelles) did not have IMF-supported programs during the 1990s.

Table 3.4. International Comparison of Trade Restrictiveness Rankings, 1998[1]

Region	Overall Rating[2]	Tariff Rating[3]	Nontariff Barrier Rating[4]
Eastern and Southern Africa	5.9	3.5	1.9
Asia, excluding fast-growing countries[5]	5.3	2.7	1.9
Fast-growing countries of Asia[5]	3.7	1.6	1.7
Eastern Europe (late transition)	4.0	2.3	1.6
Eastern Europe (early transition) and Baltic countries[6]	1.9	1.4	1.1
Former Soviet Union	3.8	1.6	1.7
Middle East and North Africa	5.5	3.1	2.0
Western Hemisphere	4.4	2.1	1.8
Industrial countries	4.0	1.2	1.9

Source: IMF staff estimates.

[1]Or latest year. In all indices, higher values denote greater restrictiveness.

[2]Index ranges from 1 to 10.

[3]Index ranges from 1 to 5.

[4]Index ranges from 1 to 3.

[5]Fast-growing countries: Hong Kong, Korea, Singapore, Thailand, Indonesia, Philippines, and Malaysia.

[6]Comprises Hungary, Poland, Czech Republic, Slovak Republic, Estonia, Latvia, and Lithuania.

while nine others had only limited restrictions (see Appendix II, Tables A5 and A6 for details of the nontariff regime as of end-1998). Thus, 14 ESA countries had few or no nontariff barriers in 1998 compared with the presence of substantial restrictive nontariff barriers in all countries at the beginning of the decade (Table 3.2). At the same time, however, the use of antidumping and safeguard measures as instruments of trade policy has received greater emphasis in the ESA region.

Several countries have adopted legislation in this area, and South Africa has significantly stepped up antidumping investigations in recent years.

• *A substantial reduction in maximum and average import tariffs.* For the region as a whole, average most-favored nation (MFN) import tariffs came down from 35 percent in the early 1990s to 15 percent in 1998, with significant decreases in Ethiopia, Kenya, Seychelles, Zambia, and the SACU

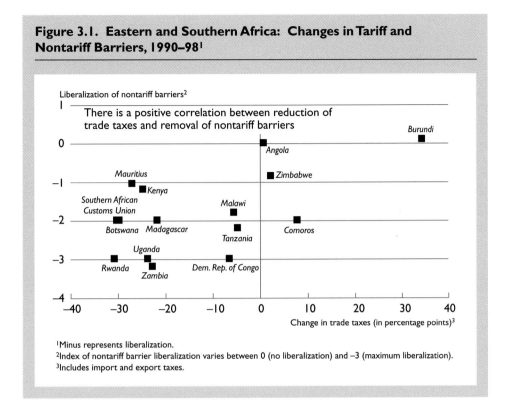

Figure 3.1. Eastern and Southern Africa: Changes in Tariff and Nontariff Barriers, 1990–98[1]

Liberalization of nontariff barriers[2]

There is a positive correlation between reduction of trade taxes and removal of nontariff barriers

Change in trade taxes (in percentage points)[3]

[1]Minus represents liberalization.
[2]Index of nontariff barrier liberalization varies between 0 (no liberalization) and –3 (maximum liberalization).
[3]Includes import and export taxes.

(Table 3.3). Maximum tariffs in the reforming countries, in many cases exceeding 100 percent at the beginning of the decade, were reduced to 25–40 percent by the end of 1998. Even some of the countries that achieved limited overall liberalization (such as Ethiopia and Kenya) brought down their maximum tariff rates considerably. The tariff reductions in reforming countries were highly correlated with reductions in nontariff barriers (Figure 3.1).

- *Reductions in effective rates of protection.* Although data on effective protection rates are not available for ESA countries except South Africa, effective protection in most countries certainly declined during the 1990s, given that top rates, usually levied on consumer goods, came down faster than lower rates, levied on intermediate and primary goods.[8] Tariff structures, however, continue to exhibit the typical cascading prop-

erty, namely, rates are higher on consumer goods than on less processed goods.

- *A simplification of the tariff regime.* With some exceptions (Burundi, Tanzania, Uganda, and Zambia), tariff regimes in the early 1990s were characterized by a large number of bands, ranging from over 10 to about 200 in the case of the SACU. In addition, many countries applied specific rates, variable duties, other duties and charges, and nontransparent valuation rules. Most of the reformers in the region simplified their systems by reducing the number of nonzero rates to less than six (Zambia, Uganda, and Kenya have just three nonzero bands),[9] thereby limiting opportunities for misclassification and fraud. Progress in improving transparency by eliminating specific rates and integrating other duties and charges in the ad valorem tariff system has, however, been mixed.

- *The reduction or elimination of export taxes.* At the beginning of the decade, almost one-half of the

---

[8]Specific revisions to tariff schedules may have prevented reductions in effective protection for important sectors of the economy. In the case of South Africa, the top rate of effective protection increased from 189 percent at the beginning of the decade to 204 percent in 1998, despite the overall trade liberalization achieved during this period.

---

[9]With the notable exception of the SACU, which had applied 72 tariff bands by end-1998.

countries in the region imposed export taxes, with collection rates ranging from 1 percent of exports in a number of countries to 21 percent in Eritrea. With the exception of Burundi and the Democratic Republic of Congo, these countries eliminated or reduced export taxes to less than 5 percent of exports during the period under review.

- *The liberalization of exchange restrictions.* With the exception of Angola and Burundi, which maintained highly restrictive systems of exchange controls, all the countries in the region substantially liberalized their exchange regimes at a relatively early stage of their reform programs. By the end of 1999, two-thirds of the countries under review had removed restrictions on current international transactions and adopted the obligations under Article VIII of the IMF's Articles of Agreement (Appendix II, Table A4).[10]

- *Reductions in exemptions.* While liberalization programs have in general been accompanied by reductions in discretionary exemptions and a broadening of the revenue base, the overall record of progress in this respect has been mixed. Even as of end–1998, in addition to certain standard (but questionable) exemptions,[11] most countries continued to grant exemptions under special investment acts and on government imports (Table 3.5). Some countries have also seen a reversal in this respect in recent years, including Mauritius, Tanzania, and Zambia.[12] Furthermore, generous exemptions were granted in efforts to promote nontraditional exports through the establishment of special tax and other incentives for exporters, including through the creation of export processing zones (EPZs). The cost of these exemptions (and of complicated tariff regimes in general) is illustrated by a measure of the collection efficiency ratio. This compares the amount a country ought to collect theoretically (given its statu-

tory tariffs) with what it actually collects. Table 3.6 shows that collection efficiency is very low in some ESA countries. Even in a well-developed country such as South Africa, the collection rate is barely 55 percent of the theoretical potential. Angola and Tanzania are extremely poor in collecting taxes. These numbers contrast with a country like Chile, whose high collection efficiency derives largely from its low and uniform tariff rate.

Despite substantial progress made by several countries, there have been a number of episodes of policy reversals, aggravating the credibility problem embedded in trade reforms.[13] Table 3.1 shows that 8 out of 22 ESA countries reversed, if only partially, the trade reforms during the 1990s. However, there were only three episodes of reversals (Malawi, Tanzania, and Zambia) among countries that undertook significant reform, and none of them was permanent.[14]

Multilateral Liberalization in Goods

In contrast to the progress made by many ESA countries in unilateral trade liberalization, they undertook very little, if any, incremental liberalization of their trade regimes under the Uruguay Round of multilateral negotiations concluded in 1994. Nor did they make substantial commitments to lock in the unilateral liberalization implemented during the 1990s by "binding" their tariffs in the WTO[15] (see Appendix II, Table A7).

In relation to industrial goods, most countries bound only a small number of tariffs, with the exception of SACU countries and Rwanda. Tariffs have been bound at very high levels, well above the actually applied rates. Thus, countries have reserved for themselves the right to reverse the trade liberalization, thereby forgoing the benefits from signaling that the reforms are irreversible. In the case of the SACU, the wedge between bound and applied tariffs is lower than the average for the region but still provides enough room for policy reversal for many products. The argument that ESA countries may not

---

[10]Zambia and Mozambique have also moved closer to Article VIII status in 1999. However, capital account liberalization has not featured prominently in the reform agenda of most countries in the region. Except for Mauritius, Uganda, and Zambia, several capital account controls are still in place in most countries.

[11]Including exemptions on imports by nongovernmental organizations and those financed by foreign donors, which usually cover a large part of total imports.

[12]In Mauritius, the share of exempted imports in total imports increased by about 10 percent during the 1990s. In Tanzania, the scope of exemptions has also increased in recent years, as evidenced by the rise in the ratio of forgone revenue relating to exemptions to total import taxes assessed (including exemptions), from 24 percent in 1993 to 48 percent in 1997–98. In Mozambique and Zambia, the authorities have emphasized recently the use of discretionary exemptions in an attempt to promote foreign investment.

---

[13]See, for instance, Rodrik (1998).

[14]Zambia introduced an across-the-board 5 percent import declaration fee in 1995 for fiscal reasons, which was eliminated in 1998. Also, an import ban on wheat flour, introduced in 1997, was lifted in the following year. The 10 percent export levy on tobacco, tea, and sugar introduced by Malawi in 1995 for fiscal reasons was eliminated in 1998. In Tanzania, some of the tariff increases in 1992 were reversed during 1993/94.[14]See, for instance, Rodrik (1998).

[15]Binding represents a legal commitment by a country not to raise tariffs above a specified level. If a binding is breached by a country it has to compensate partner countries or face retaliation by them.

Table 3.5. Selected ESA Countries: Status of Tariff Exemptions, December 1998

	Government	Public Enterprises	Investment Convention or Code	NGOs	Foreign-Financed Projects	Other[1]
Angola	Yes	No	Yes	Yes	Yes	Yes
Burundi	Yes	Yes	Yes	Yes	Yes	Yes
Congo, Dem. Rep. of	Yes	No	Yes	Yes	Yes	Yes
Comoros	Yes	No	Yes	Yes	Yes	Yes
Ethiopia	Yes	No	No	Yes	Yes	Yes
Kenya	No	No	Yes	Yes	Yes	Yes
Lesotho	No	No	No	Yes	No	No
Madagascar	Yes	No	Yes	Yes	Yes	Yes
Malawi	No	No	No	Yes	Yes	Yes
Mauritius	No	No	Yes	Yes	Yes	Yes
Mozambique	No	No	Yes	Yes	No	Yes
Namibia	Yes	No	Yes	Yes	Yes	Yes
Rwanda	Yes	Yes	Yes	Yes	Yes	Yes
Seychelles	Yes	Yes	Yes	Yes	Yes	Yes
Swaziland	No	No	No	Yes	No	No
Tanzania	Yes	Yes	Yes	Yes	Yes	No
Uganda	No	No	No	No	No	No
Zambia	No	No	Yes	Yes	Yes	Yes
Zimbabwe	Yes	No	Yes	Yes	Yes	Yes

Source: IMF, African Department.
[1]Includes discretionary exemptions and waivers.

have anticipated the liberalization that they would undertake independently of the Uruguay Round and, hence, did not bind their tariffs at reasonable levels is difficult to sustain. This is because the wedge, even for early 1990s tariff levels, is very large (except for the SACU), provoking the question as to

Table 3.6. International Comparison of Tariff Collection Efficiency, 1996[1]
(Percent)

Country	Collection Efficiency
Angola	36.0
Malawi	47.2
Mauritius	56.1
South Africa	54.7
Tanzania	38.1
Zimbabwe	53.1
New Zealand	84.0
Chile	76.0

Source: World Bank (1999).
[1]Measured as the ratio of the duties collected on imports to the import-weighted tariff.

why these countries did not bind tariffs at or close to the then prevailing tariff levels. In relation to agricultural goods, all countries were required to bind tariffs and all other charges on imports. While ESA countries have complied with this requirement, they have nevertheless bound their tariffs and charges at extremely high levels, often in excess of 100 percent, diluting the value of the commitments made to their trading partners.

Liberalization in Services

It is increasingly recognized that trade in services represents the next frontier of liberalization. Between 1980 and 1998, the value of world trade in services increased by 252 percent, as against 164 percent for trade in goods. Furthermore, many of the technological advances witnessed in recent years have been related to the services sectors—transportation, telecommunications, and financial services are seen as crucial to improving competitiveness because they provide inputs to manufacturing and other export-oriented activities. In many traded goods, services account for more than half of input costs.

Table 3.7. Eastern and Southern Africa: Banking Sector Structure and Liberalization, December 1997

Country	Concentration Index[1]	Presence of Foreign Banks in Five Largest Banks	
		Number	Share of loans and deposits
Angola	0.29	2	27
Botswana	0.30	5	100
Congo, Dem. Rep. of	0.26	5	100
Comoros	1.00	5	100
Eritrea	0.75	0	0
Ethiopia	0.81	0	0
Kenya	0.23	2	45
Lesotho	0.48	0	0
Madagascar	0.24	3	47
Malawi	0.76	1	4
Mauritius	0.44	3	20
Mozambique	0.33	5	100
Namibia	0.27	5	100
South Africa	0.25	0	0
Swaziland	0.21	4	88
Tanzania	0.47	3	27
Uganda	0.59	2	80
Zambia	0.26	3	51
Zimbabwe	0.22	3	57
Average	0.43	3	50

Source: Gelbard and Leite (1999).
[1]Herfindahl index of concentration.

Table 3.8. International Comparison of Liberalization of the Banking Industry: Developing Country Members of the WTO

	WTO Members[1]	Members Making Commitments[2]	Liberalization Index	
			Simple average	GDP-weighted
Africa	41 (1.5)	13 (80)	0.68	0.57
Of which: Eastern and Southern Africa	18 (0.7)	8 (88)	0.65	0.62
Asia	25 (7.6)	17 (95)	0.28	0.33
Europe	7 (1.1)	7 (100)	0.60	0.61
Latin America	32 (6.2)	18 (97)	0.38	0.34
All	105 (16.4)	55 (95)	0.37	0.37

Source: Mattoo (1999).
[1]Numbers in brackets represent the fraction of GDP of all WTO members.
[2]Numbers in brackets represent the fraction of GDP of members in that regional grouping.

While liberalization of trade in goods depends on, and is measured as, openness to foreign competition, liberalization in services needs to take into account two additional factors—the domestic market structure and the nature of regulation. The efficiency benefits of liberalizing services sectors derive from the extent of competition, the extent of foreign direct investment, which brings in improved technology and managerial know-how, and the effectiveness of regulation. The latter is important, particularly where markets are imperfectly competitive and where monopoly incumbents' control of access to essential facilities can deter entry by competitors (see Mattoo and others, 2000). In these cases, regulation can promote competition, enabling the efficiency benefits to be realized.

Little information is available on the extent to which the services sector is protected in ESA countries and the ensuing efficiency losses. One crude measure of how much liberalization has been undertaken by ESA countries is the number of sectors in which they made commitments in the WTO (see Appendix II, Table A8). South Africa and Lesotho were the two countries that undertook the most commitments, as measured by the number of sectors covered—9 and 10, respectively, out of a maximum of 12 sectors. They were followed by Burundi, Kenya, Mauritius, and Rwanda, which committed to liberalization in 5 sectors. Most commitments were in the area of tourism (16 countries), followed by business services (10 countries), financial services (8), and communications (7).

While the services sector comprises a wide range of activities, two sectors that are considered critical in creating a favorable climate for investment and facilitating growth are banking and telecommunications. There is substantial participation of foreign banks in ESA countries' banking systems (the share of loans and deposits of foreign banks in the total amount of loans and deposits of the five largest banks averages 50 percent). In most countries, however, the structure of the banking system is excessively concentrated, as measured by the Herfindahl index of concentration[16] (Table 3.7). Furthermore, there is a need to improve the institutional and regulatory environment of most ESA countries, particularly with respect to judicial loan recovery, enforcement of financial contracts, property transfers, and

adoption of modern commercial legislation (Gelbard and Leite, 1999).

Table 3.8 contains data on liberalization commitments relating to the banking sector undertaken by all developing country members of the WTO. Of the 18 WTO members in the ESA region, only eight countries—Angola, Kenya, Lesotho, Malawi, Mauritius, Mozambique, South Africa, and Zimbabwe—undertook any commitment, a lower share than in any region outside Africa (column 2). Columns 3–4 describe the nature of liberalization commitments undertaken by these countries, measured by an index computed by Mattoo (1999). The higher the value of the index, the less the liberalization undertaken in the WTO.[17] The value of the index for ESA is substantially higher than the average for all countries. The eight countries in the ESA that did undertake commitments in the financial services sector bound them at a more restrictive level than all groupings outside Africa. Only African countries outside ESA were more restrictive than ESA countries.

Table 3.9 describes both the unilateral and multilateral liberalization efforts of ESA countries in the telecommunications sector. The left-hand panel of the table shows the WTO commitments undertaken by ESA countries in the telecommunications sector—only 5 of the 20 countries shown in the table have undertaken any commitments, and even these countries have essentially codified the existing policy framework with little new or incremental liberalization. The actual openness of the sector is summarized in the right-hand panel of the table. Of the 20 ESA countries shown, 16 countries have a monopoly supplier of telecommunications services in the three main market segments (local, local long distance, and international). These monopoly suppliers tend to be publicly owned, with foreign participation in only 3 countries—South Africa, Uganda, and Madagascar—and majority foreign ownership in only 1 country. It is now recognized that sound regulation ensuring a competitive market structure is an essential complement to foreign ownership in fostering an efficient sector. On this score too, ESA countries are lagging behind. Of the 20 ESA countries, very few have a statutorily independent regulator.

---

[16]Computed as $H_i = \sum_{j=1,\ldots 5}(S_j/\sum_{j=1,\ldots 5}S_j)^2$, where S_j is the sum of deposits and loans for bank j. As defined, the index equals one in the case of a monopoly and 0 in the case of equal shares. An index value higher than 0.3 is normally associated with an imperfect market structure.

[17]The liberalization index corresponds to the bound rather than the applied level of access, and, therefore, does not necessarily correlate with how liberal actual conditions are.

Table 3.9. Eastern and Southern Africa: Telecommunications Liberalization

| | Commitments in the WTO | | | | | Features of Sector | | | | | |
| | Commitments on cross-border supply | | Commitments on inward foreign investment | | Adherence to pro-competitive regulatory principles | Degree of market liberalization | | | Foreign ownership (percent) | Domestic ownership | Comments |
	Full	Limited	Full	No. of Suppliers		Local	Local long distance	International long distance			
Kenya		Yes	No	1	Yes	Monopoly	Monopoly	Monopoly	30	Public	
Mauritius		Yes	No	1	Yes	Monopoly	Monopoly	Monopoly	0	Public	
South Africa		Yes	No	1	Yes	Monopoly	Monopoly	Monopoly	0	Public	
Uganda		Yes	No	2	Yes	Duopoly	Duopoly	Duopoly	0–90	Public/private	
Zimbabwe	Yes		No			Monopoly	Monopoly	Monopoly	0	Public	50 percent foreign ownership allowed
Angola						Monopoly	Monopoly	Monopoly	0	Public	
Botswana						Monopoly	Monopoly	Monopoly	0	Public	
Burundi						Monopoly	Monopoly	Monopoly	0	Public	
Congo, Dem. Rep. of						Partial competition	Partial competition	Partial competition	0	Public	
Eritrea						Monopoly	Monopoly	Monopoly	0	Public	45 percent foreign ownership allowed
Ethiopia						Monopoly	Monopoly	Monopoly	0	Public	
Lesotho						Monopoly	Monopoly	Monopoly	0	Public	
Madagascar						Partial competition	Partial competition	Partial competition	66	Public	
Malawi						Monopoly	Monopoly	Monopoly	0	Public	
Mozambique						Monopoly	Monopoly	Monopoly	0	Public	50 percent foreign ownership allowed
Namibia						Monopoly	Monopoly	Monopoly	0	Public	49 percent foreign ownership allowed
Rwanda						Monopoly	Monopoly	Monopoly	1	Public	
Swaziland						Monopoly	Monopoly	Monopoly	0	Public	
Tanzania						Partial competition	Partial competition	Partial competition	0	Public	65 percent foreign ownership allowed
Zambia						Monopoly	Monopoly	Monopoly	0	Public	

Sources: Schedules submitted to the WTO; and ITU (1999).

IV   Regional Integration

Preferential Liberalization in Goods

During the 1990s, in addition to the Cross-Border Initiative, countries in eastern and southern Africa embarked on a number of bilateral and regional trade arrangements (RTAs). These arrangements include COMESA, SADC, SACU, EAC, and the IOC. There is also the free trade agreement between the European Union (EU) and South Africa, that presages significant preferential liberalization on the north-south axis; the recent accord between ACP countries (African, Caribbean, and Pacific) and the EU, that extends for a considerable period the concessions of the Lomé conventions; and the African Growth and Opportunity Act that provides for duty-free treatment of Sub-Saharan African exports to the United States.

The member states of COMESA (consisting of 18 ESA countries plus Djibouti, Egypt, and Sudan) have been implementing phased preferential reductions in import tariffs in recent years with the objective of achieving a free trade area by October 2000. The aim is to establish a customs union by 2004, in which there will be a common external tariff structure with a small number of tariff bands. So far, progress on intraregional tariff liberalization has been mixed. As of March 1, 1999, only Egypt and Madagascar met the targeted 90 percent margin. Eight countries (Comoros, Eritrea, Kenya, Mauritius, Sudan, Tanzania,[18] Uganda, and Zimbabwe) had agreed to an 80 percent preferential margin, and Malawi to a 70 percent margin. In addition, three countries (Burundi, Rwanda, and Zambia) had offered a 60 percent margin. Seven countries (Angola, Democratic Republic of Congo, Djibouti, Ethiopia, Namibia, Swaziland, and Seychelles) had not made any preferential tariff reductions, although Namibia and Swaziland were given derogations because of their membership in SACU, and Djibouti did not levy discriminatory import taxes. Both the EAC and the IOC support the effort of their members to abide by the trade liberalization goals of COMESA.

Over half of the countries in COMESA also participate in the CBI, which encourages a "fast track" to trade liberalization. The CBI originally sought to establish free trade among participating countries and a harmonized external tariff by October 1998. External tariffs were to have no more than three nonzero rates, a maximum rate of 20–25 percent (including all import taxes), a difference between the lowest and the highest rate of no more than 20 percentage points, and a weighted-average rate of less than 15 percent. Although none of the CBI countries met the target for eliminating intraregional tariffs, 10 of the 14 countries implemented preference margins of 60–80 percent by end-1998. Outcomes on external tariff reductions have also fallen short of the targets; Zambia and Uganda are the only two countries that have met the agreed targets. However, most CBI countries achieved significant progress in eliminating nontariff barriers, reducing the monopoly power on trade of state marketing boards or state enterprises, liberalizing foreign exchange regimes and domestic financial markets, harmonizing road transit charges, and introducing a single goods customs declaration form. In some cases, there was also significant progress in simplifying investment procedures, particularly through the establishment of a one-stop investment approval authority. Since May 2000, the CBI changed its name to Regional Integration Facilitation Forum (RIFF), refocusing its activities on investment facilitation while at the same time broadening its agenda to include other issues related to regional macroeconomic developments and cooperation among the RTAs.

Although the SADC free trade protocol was signed in 1996 and has been ratified by most countries,[19] details have not been agreed on how nontariff barriers and intraregional tariffs will be phased out within the eight-year period, expected to begin

---

[18]Tanzania will withdraw from COMESA effective September 2000.

[19]Angola, the Democratic Republic of Congo, and the Seychelles are the only three countries that are not signatories of the protocol, though Angola and Seychelles have signaled their intention to accede to it in the near future.

in September 2000, for the establishment of a free trade area. Three classes of products have been defined according to the speed of liberalization: immediate, gradual, and sensitive products. For goods in the latter category (including textiles and automotive products), tariffs will only come down at the end of the eight-year period. The more developed member countries (South Africa and its SACU partners) will reduce their tariffs on imports faster than other SADC countries, and tariffs on imports of non-SACU countries from BLNS (Botswana, Lesotho, Namibia, and Swaziland) countries will fall faster than tariffs on imports from South Africa. There is no plan for a concerted reduction in external tariffs, which are widely different across SADC countries. However, product-specific rules of origin determining the domestic content requirements for a large number of products are being considered, including a 100 percent domestic content requirement for (primarily agricultural) inputs that are produced within SADC.

Members of these RTAs are also trying to foster economic integration by other mechanisms in addition to tariff reductions. The SADC, for instance, is developing policies and stimulating joint projects and standards across areas such as transport, power generation, water, human resource development, and finance and investment. COMESA has streamlined customs procedures, promoted cross-border vehicle licensing and insurance, and is working to facilitate cross-border payments and settlements. However, there is considerable overlap in the membership of these arrangements, giving rise to a number of problems discussed in Section VII below.

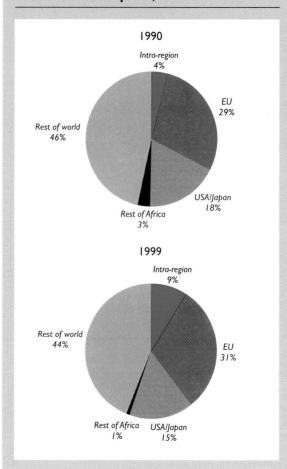

Figure 4.1. Eastern and Southern Africa: Destination of Exports, 1990 and 1999

Trade Developments

Owing primarily to its size but also to its more advanced level of industrial development, South Africa accounts for more than 70 percent of the imports of other countries in the ESA region. This leads to a large trade surplus with the region of about US$4 billion. The BLNS countries, Malawi, Mozambique, Zambia, and Zimbabwe exhibit a high degree of reliance on South Africa for their total imports, ranging from 35 percent to 60 percent, and only Zimbabwe sells more than 20 percent of its exports to South Africa.

Trade links among ESA countries have intensified in recent years: the share of intraregional exports in total exports increased from 4 percent in 1990 to 9 percent in 1999 (Figure 4.1). This increase in intraregional trade reflects predominantly the intensification of links with South Africa following the

demise of the apartheid regime, as there was a small decline in intraregional trade among ESA countries excluding the SACU countries (see Table 4.1). The share of imports from industrial countries has declined for all countries except SACU and Madagascar, as South Africa has displaced some of their products, and there has been an increase in South African exports to the EU.

Within ESA, regional links are most intense within SADC followed by the CBI and COMESA (Appendix II, Tables A9–A11). In 1999, about 10 percent of total SADC trade was intraregional, compared with 6 percent for COMESA. These links have also intensified over time in SADC, as the share of intraregional imports in total imports grew from about 5 percent in 1990 to 12 percent in 1999. By contrast, intra-COMESA trade has remained virtually unchanged during this period.

Table 4.1. Eastern and Southern Africa: Intraregional and Extraregional Trade with Selected Partners

	Imports			Exports		
	1990	1994	1999	1990	1994	1999
	(Millions of U.S. dollars)					
ESA trade						
Intraregional[1]	2,255	4,066	5,963	1,640	3,882	5,614
By SACU from/to rest of ESA region	79	573	596	405	2,257	3,561
By rest of ESA region from/to SACU	982	2,290	3,744	174	454	557
Between rest of ESA region	1,194	1,203	1,623	1,062	1,171	1,496
Extraregional	43,020	46,486	65,779	38,064	38,010	56,925
Rest of Africa	735	333	423	1,247	470	640
EU	19,002	19,237	28,003	11,324	10,648	19,164
United States	4,698	6,551	7,412	4,804	4,492	7,012
Japan	3,203	3,757	3,669	2,259	1,787	2,793
Rest of world	15,382	16,609	26,272	18,431	20,613	27,316
Total	45,275	50,552	71,741	39,704	41,892	62,539
	(Percent of total)					
ESA trade						
Intraregional	5.0	8.0	8.3	4.1	9.3	9.0
By SACU from/to rest of ESA region	0.2	1.1	0.8	1.0	5.4	5.7
By rest of ESA region from/to SACU	2.2	4.5	5.2	0.4	1.1	0.9
Between rest of ESA region	2.6	2.4	2.3	2.7	2.8	2.4
Extraregional	95.0	92.0	91.7	95.9	90.7	91.0
Rest of Africa	1.6	0.7	0.6	3.1	1.1	1.0
EU	42.0	38.1	39.0	28.5	25.4	30.6
United States	10.4	13.0	10.3	12.1	10.7	11.2
Japan	7.1	7.4	5.1	5.7	4.3	4.5
Rest of world	34.0	32.9	36.6	46.4	49.2	43.7
Total	100	100	100	100	100	100
	(Percent of GDP)					
Memorandum items						
Intraregional	1.2	2.0	2.8	0.9	2.0	2.7
Extraregional	22.4	23.4	31.4	19.8	19.1	27.2
Total	23.6	25.4	34.3	20.7	21.1	29.9

Source: IMF, *Direction of Trade Statistics.*

[1]Import and export data differ mainly because partner country data are used directly or indirectly in estimating missing figures. Imports are measured c.i.f.; exports are measured f.o.b.

V   The External Environment and Trade Developments

External Environment

ESA countries faced changes in their external environment in the 1990s, caused by the increasing trend toward globalization and worldwide trade liberalization, most notably as a result of the conclusion of the Uruguay Round. These changes had four implications for ESA countries' trading opportunities. Two of these relate to the preferential market access enjoyed by ESA countries and the other two to nonpreferential access.

- First, the effect of the tariff reductions implemented in the Uruguay Round was to reduce the margin of preferences enjoyed by ESA countries in industrial countries' markets.[20] The magnitude of the losses for ESA countries has been estimated, however, to be relatively small, varying between 0.1 percent and 0.5 percent of their exports (Appendix II, Table A12).[21]

- Second, perhaps a more important source of disruption for ESA countries is the reduction in preferential access on items such as beef, sugar, and textiles, which these countries enjoy in the form of guaranteed quotas, particularly in the EU market. In the case of beef and sugar, there are reduced rents accruing to ESA countries' exporters. In the case of textiles, the loss could be even more severe if ESA countries fail to adapt to the competitive conditions that would arise from the elimination of quotas on textiles and clothing products. For example, Mauritius,

which has sizable exports of these products, could well face severe competition from lower cost suppliers in Asia, threatening its current market niche.

- Third, tariff reductions by industrial countries on tropical commodities will benefit ESA countries, but the effect is expected to be small as these commodities were already subject to very low tariffs prior to the Uruguay Round (Harrold, 1995).

- Lastly, as a result of the tariff cuts under the Uruguay Round, the tariff escalation faced by ESA countries has been reduced to some extent, although it will endure for a number of important products (wood, textiles and clothing, fish, and leather).[22] Tariff escalation has the effect of encouraging exports of raw materials from ESA countries rather than products higher up the value-added chain, thereby militating against diversification and industrialization in those countries (Harrold, 1995).

Openness

During the 1990s, there was an appreciable increase in the openness of ESA countries as measured by the ratios of exports and imports of goods and services to GDP (Figure 5.1). Between 1990 and 1999, the average trade-GDP ratio increased by 9 percentage points, although wide variations existed between countries in the region, and eight countries actually experienced a decline in their trade-to-GDP ratios (Table 5.1). These developments reflected the extent of trade liberalization in the region and resulted in higher merchandise trade, rather than trade in services. On average, the share of trade in nonfactor services in GDP remained broadly unchanged at about 30 percent.

A statistical analysis of the determinants of the openness of ESA countries reveals that trade liberal-

---

[20]ESA countries that are net importers of foodstuffs could also be affected by the increase in prices brought about by the reduction in subsidization of agricultural products. This increase is, however, expected to be small.

[21]These preferences stem from various arrangements between industrial countries and ESA countries, such as the Generalized System of Preferences between the European Union, Japan, and the United States, on the one hand, and developing countries, on the other. There are also the Lomé Convention, involving the EU and several low-income countries, including ESA countries, and others, such as the Multi-Fiber Arrangement, under which several ESA countries have special quotas for the export of textiles and clothing products.

[22]Tariff escalation is a phenomenon whereby tariffs increase with the stage of processing.

Figure 5.1. Eastern and Southern Africa: Imports and Exports, 1990 and 1999
(Percent of GDP)

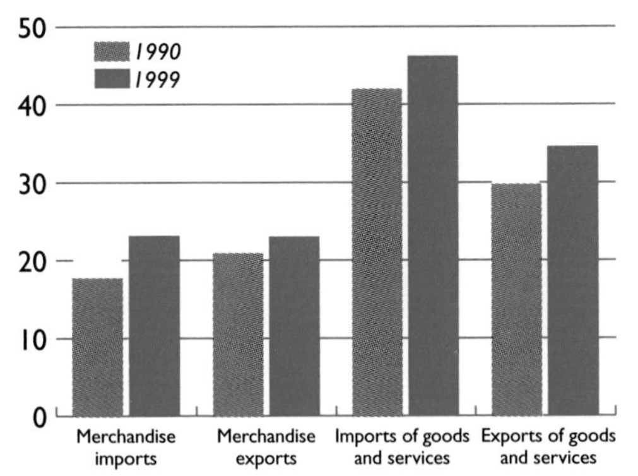

izing was one of the factors behind the observed increase in openness during the 1990s (Box 5.1). On average, a 1 percent reduction in trade taxes led to an increase in the trade-to-GDP ratio of about 0.9 percentage points, and the corresponding coefficients were statistically significant.

Export Performance

Export performance of ESA countries lagged behind that of the rest of the world, particularly other developing countries. The average annual growth in export volume for ESA countries was 5.4 percent, compared with 6.4 percent for the world as a whole. However, there was a substantial pick-up in exports in the second half of the 1990s, with export growth of 6.4 percent, compared with 4.5 percent between 1990 and 1994. Within ESA, a few countries—Ethiopia, Lesotho, Madagascar, Mozambique, Seychelles, and Uganda—registered impres-

Table 5.1. Eastern and Southern Africa: Openness Indicators, 1990 and 1999
(Percent of GDP)

	Exports of Goods and Services		Imports of Goods and Services		Total Trade	
	1990	1999	1990	1999	1990	1999
Angola	39	78	23	56	62	133
Botswana	53	48	53	48	106	95
Burundi	8	5	28	15	36	20
Comoros	14	22	37	49	51	71
Ethiopia	8	13	12	29	20	42
Kenya	26	26	31	34	57	59
Lesotho	24	28	120	101	144	129
Madagascar	17	25	27	34	44	59
Malawi	26	30	31	40	57	69
Mauritius	63	64	71	60	134	124
Mozambique	9	13	34	40	43	53
Namibia	52	53	68	64	120	118
Rwanda	6	5	14	21	20	26
Seychelles	70	69	72	68	141	136
South Africa	24	25	23	23	47	48
Swaziland	77	86	88	102	165	188
Tanzania	20	14	33	30	52	44
Uganda	6	13	17	32	23	44
Zambia	36	30	37	40	72	70
Zimbabwe	23	46	23	41	46	87
ESA[1]	30	35	42	46	72	81
ESA (excl. South Africa)[1]	30	35	43	47	73	82
Sub-Saharan Africa[1]	28	30	27	32	55	61

Source: IMF staff estimates.

[1]All averages are unweighted and exclude the DRC and Eritrea.

Box 5.1. Trade Protection and Trade Outcomes in Africa

Is trade in Africa determined exclusively by exogenous factors, such as geography, or does trade policy play an important role? To examine this question, and consistent with the approach in Rodrik (1999), a set of regressions was run on a sample of 37 sub-Saharan African countries for the period 1984–98. To provide a suitably large data set for the analysis, the sample was split into two time periods, 1984–91 and 1992–98. The dependent variable was the ratio of exports and imports to GDP or the ratio of exports to GDP (the trade outcome variable), and the independent variables included the log of initial per capita income (logincome) and population (logpop), a measure of the proportion of a country's land area in the tropics (tropics), trade taxes (tradetax), import taxes (importax), and export taxes (exportax). The tax variables were measured in terms of collections: for example, import taxes were measured as customs duty collections divided by the value of imports. Timedum is a dummy variable aimed at capturing

any structural shifts across the two time periods. The results are presented in the table below.

The regressions show that trade and export outcomes are determined by income levels, geographical variables, *and* trade policy. The fit of the regressions, particularly for this type of cross-section analysis, is quite good. The coefficients on the size variables (income and population) are usually significant at the 5 percent level and are correctly signed. They were also quite robust to alternative specifications. More important, the trade policy variables also turned out to be significant, robust, and correctly signed. The results suggest that a 1 percentage point reduction in trade taxes leads to a trade increase of between 0.7 and 1.1 percentage points. Interestingly, and consistent with Lerner's theoretical proposition that import taxes are equivalent to export taxes in terms of their relative price and resource allocation effects, the coefficients on the two tax terms turn out to be broadly similar.

	(X+M)/GDP	X/GDP	X/GDP
Logincome	7.94 **	7.47 ***	9.66 ***
Logpop	−6.89 **	−2.63 *	−1.40
Tropics	−67.06 ***	−14.06 **	−8.12
Tradetax		−0.88 ***	
Importax	−0.71 ***		−0.41 **
Exportax	−0.44 ***		−0.25 ***
Timedum	Yes	Yes	Yes
N	48	48	41
R²	0.81	0.54	0.46

Note: ***, **, and * denote significance at the 10 percent, 5 percent, and 1 percent levels, respectively.
X: value of exports.
M: value of imports.

sive export performance, comparable to that of other fast growing developing countries (Table 5.2). For ESA countries (as for sub-Saharan Africa in general), the growth of exports of manufactures was relatively strong, with the share in total exports increasing from 28 percent in 1985 to about 37 percent in 1996.[23] Particularly striking was the performance of Madagascar, Uganda, and the SACU countries (Appendix II, Table A13). The share of traditional exports—encompassing agricultural ma-

terials, fuels, ores, and metals—all decreased relative to the late 1980s. Within manufacturing, the sector exhibiting the most dynamic growth was clothing (Appendix II, Table A14). However, the export performance of countries in the ESA region has been negatively affected by anticompetitive arrangements in the transportation and insurance sectors, as reflected in the relatively high level of freight costs that exceed the level of tariff barriers by a wide margin.[24]

---

[23]This result is based on Yeats (1998) and covers eight ESA countries for which reliable data are available at a disaggregated level. The countries are Kenya, Madagascar, Malawi, Mauritius, South Africa, Uganda, Zambia, and Zimbabwe. The non-ESA sub-Saharan African countries covered are Benin, Burkina Faso, Cameroon, Gabon, Côte d'Ivoire, and Senegal.

[24]According to Amjadi and Yeats (1995), net payments on freight and insurance by sub-Saharan African countries were in 1990–91 equivalent to about 15 percent of exports of goods and services, more than twice as high as in other developing countries. In landlocked countries such as Malawi and Uganda, the ratio was well above 50 percent.

Table 5.2. Eastern and Southern Africa: Growth in Export Volume

Country	Average Annual Rate of Growth		
	1990–94	1995–99	1990–99
Angola	2.5	7.3	4.9
Botswana	4.1	3.6	3.9
Burundi	–2.5	10.3	3.9
Comoros	1.0	2.0	1.5
Congo, Democratic Republic of	–14.7	3.6	–5.6
Ethiopia	5.6	10.8	8.2
Kenya	7.3	3.1	5.2
Lesotho	28.0	3.8	15.9
Madagascar	4.1	9.9	7.0
Malawi	7.2	5.9	6.6
Mauritius	1.0	2.3	1.7
Mozambique	10.0	9.5	9.7
Namibia	0.7	2.1	1.4
Rwanda	–8.5	8.7	0.1
Seychelles	16.4	26.6	21.5
South Africa	3.6	4.9	4.2
Swaziland	6.4	3.9	5.1
Tanzania	5.8	0.0	2.9
Uganda	15.4	16.0	15.7
Zambia	–0.8	–1.1	–1.0
Zimbabwe	2.5	0.9	0.9
All countries	4.5	6.4	5.4
All countries, exc. South Africa	4.6	6.5	5.5
Sub-Saharan Africa	3.4	5.5	4.3

Source: Country authorities and IMF staff estimates.

increase in the number of items exported, among which Zambia stands out as a strong performer (Appendix II, Table A15). On related measures of diversification—the single- and three-product concentration ratios[25]—ESA countries' performance was positive, with the concentration ratios falling in six of the eight countries. The performance of ESA countries contrasts sharply with that of six other sub-Saharan African countries investigated, which showed a marked decrease in the level of diversification measured on all three counts (the number of products exported and the one- and three-product concentration ratios).

One of the key aspects of globalization has been the recent trend toward increased specialization at the level of the firm, the plant, and product lines—as reflected in increasing intra-industry trade. This specialization has also led to the phenomenon of global production sharing, whereby different components of a good are produced in various geographical locations. With the exception of South Africa, however, most African countries have insignificant levels of intra-industry trade, reflecting their low level of industrialization and the limited degree of regional vertical integration (Appendix II, Table A16). Even South Africa ranks only in the middle of emerging market countries—Brazil, Taiwan, Province of China, and Korea have intra-industry trade ratios that are nearly twice as large. Similarly, apart from South Africa, there has been no discernible dynamism in trade in parts and components in the other ESA countries.

This aggregate manufacturing export performance was accompanied by a small increase in the diversity of products exported by ESA countries. Four of the eight ESA countries studied showed an

---

[25]The single-product and three-product concentration ratios measure the share of total exports accounted for by the largest and the three largest export items, respectively.

VI   Macroeconomic Aspects of Trade Liberalization

This section deals with two questions: whether initial macroeconomic conditions influenced the extent of trade liberalization during the 1990s, and whether trade liberalization was associated in identifiable ways with the macroeconomic performance of ESA countries.[26] The description below does not purport to assign causality: there is the customary difficulty of isolating the impact of macroeconomic conditions on trade liberalization from other factors, and vice versa. The analysis aims at highlighting the stylized aspects of the relation between macroeconomic conditions and trade liberalization, drawing upon the experience of individual countries.

Countries are classified into two groups according to the level of trade liberalization achieved at the end of 1998.[27] Countries that by 1998 had lowered their index of trade restrictiveness to 4 or less are classified as part of the "substantial liberalization" group (i.e., the bottom two categories in Table 3.1, also referred to as fast reformers), while the remaining countries are placed in the "moderate-or-no-liberalization" (i.e., the top two categories in Table 3.1, also referred to as slow reformers) group.

Initial Macroeconomic Conditions

Initial macroeconomic conditions do not appear to have played a decisive role in ESA governments' decisions to liberalize trade (Zimbabwe is one country where macroeconomic factors may have played a role in slowing, even reversing, liberalization). Countries in the moderate-or-no-liberalization group did not display consistently larger macroeconomic imbal-

ances in the early 1990s. At the same time, a number of ambitious reformers—Uganda, Zambia, Mozambique—faced severe macroeconomic imbalances in the early 1990s, with inflation rates varying between 36 and 135 percent and very high fiscal and current account deficits. Far from constraining reform, these imbalances may even have provided a spur to the reform process.

The substantial liberalization group had larger initial current account deficits than the slow liberalizers, but managed to improve their external position over the 1990s. The average current account deficit declined by about 4 percentage points for the former set of countries, but deteriorated by a further 2 percentage points for the latter. This may have resulted in part from better exchange rate management. Countries that liberalized, on average, saw their real effective exchange rate depreciate by about 6 percent (cumulatively) during the period 1990–98, while that of the slow reformers appreciated by about 11 percent. The six countries—Angola, Congo, Eritrea, Kenya, Rwanda, and Tanzania—that experienced the most adverse movements in the exchange rate were in the group of slow liberalizers. Thus, to some extent, a depreciating exchange rate in liberalizing countries may have averted or mitigated short-term pressures on their external position.

Trade Liberalization and Macroeconomic Outcomes

Even though not every country in the "substantial liberalization" group had a superior economic performance during the 1993–99 period, the figures show that these countries have, on average, fared much better than the countries in the "moderate-or-no-liberalization" group. This is particularly the case for GDP growth, investment ratios, and fiscal and inflation performance (Appendix II, Table A18). In the case of South Africa, there is evidence that trade liberalization contributed to the dynamic efficiency of the economy, as reflected in faster growth of total factor productivity (Box 6.1).

---

[26]The following variables are analyzed: GDP growth, GDP per capita growth, growth in export volume, inflation performance, the fiscal balances, the current account balance (the latter two excluding grants and expressed as a share of GDP), and indicators of trade revenue dependency. The Democratic Republic of Congo and Eritrea are excluded from the analysis because their macroeconomic data are either unavailable or highly distorted by the recent wars in these countries.

[27]In virtually all cases, those countries that had open trade regimes in 1998 were also the ones that undertook the most liberalization since the beginning of the decade.

Box 6.1. South Africa: Dynamic Gains From Trade Liberalization

South Africa undertook significant trade liberalization in the 1990s and has experienced a large increase in the openness of its economy. The impetus for liberalization started gaining momentum in the late 1980s, reflected in a consultative process under the auspices of the tripartite National Economic Forum involving government, labor, and organized business. As a result, South Africa adopted a two-pronged approach to trade liberalization, consisting of multilateral trade liberalization in the context of the Uruguay Round of trade negotiations and unilateral trade liberalization. Neither fiscal nor macroeconomic considerations influenced trade reform in South Africa. Trade taxes accounted for a very small share of total revenue—and in any event much of the revenue derived from trade was transferred to SACU partners. Furthermore, inflation steadily declined during the 1990s while the external position—although subject to episodic shocks—was generally sound.

Virtually all quantitative restrictions have now been eliminated, including those operating through agricultural marketing boards. The tariff regime has been rationalized, with the number of lines reduced from over 13,000 in 1993 to about 7,900 in 1998 and the number of tariff bands reduced from well over 100 to 72. These data mask the progress made in reducing the actual complexity of the tariff regime, as the number of lines carrying formula duties (that acted like variable import levies) was reduced from 1,900 in 1993 to 28 in 1997 and the number of lines facing specific tariffs was reduced from 500 to 227. The standard deviation of tariffs declined from 43 to about 15, while the range of effective protection was also narrowed.

In a recent study, Jonsson and Subramanian (2000) show that South Africa's increased openness and the recent trade liberalization have had a beneficial impact on

dynamic efficiency in the 1990s, in particular on growth in total factor productivity (TPF). The study uses both a time-series approach at the aggregate level and a cross-section approach across different manufacturing sectors. Both approaches yield results supportive of a strong and statistically robust relationship between trade and total factor productivity. Furthermore, this improvement in overall efficiency was not a consequence of reduced employment levels.

The time-series analysis yields a co-integrating relationship between TFP, openness (defined as the sum of exports and imports of goods and nonfactor services divided by GDP), and the share of machinery and equipment in total investment, with the evidence suggesting that causality runs from openness to TFP. On average, a 1 percentage point increase in openness results in a long-run increase in annual TFP growth of about 0.5 percent. Similarly, an increase in the share of investment in machinery and equipment of 10 percentage points is associated with higher TFP growth of about 3 percentage points. Furthermore, both the openness and the investment in machinery and equipment variable are important for the co-integration result, indicating that the two sources complement each other in influencing productivity. Although research and development (R&D) augments productivity, it is also important to provide an open and liberal environment in which gains from R&D can be maximized.

In the cross-section analysis, the trade variable is measured in terms of domestic policy liberalization and the results indicate that those manufacturing subsectors that witnessed greater trade liberalization during the 1990s achieved higher TFP growth. On average, a 10 percent reduction in prices induced by trade liberalization in a sector, led to a 3 percent increase in its annual TFP growth.

Typically, countries in the "substantial liberalization" group embraced a wider range of economic reforms during the 1990s than countries in the other group. This is important insofar as trade liberalization is likely to be just one of the factors affecting economic performance, and trade reforms are likely to be more successful in an environment where a comprehensive set of reforms is in place or being implemented. Mozambique (Box 6.2) and Uganda provide positive evidence on the impact on growth of bold and comprehensive reforms. Countries that had problems implementing comprehensive reforms experienced macroeconomic instability that undermined any positive effects of trade liberalization on economic growth (for example, Zambia, Box 6.3).

Per capita GDP growth was also—on average—higher in the "substantial liberalization" group than

in the "moderate-or-no-liberalization" group (Figure 6.1). Growth in export volumes was also positively correlated with trade liberalization when countries affected by war were excluded, and current account balances in most liberalizing countries improved, while the opposite was true for countries with little or no liberalization (Figure 6.2).

Mauritius is an interesting case because it registered high rates of export and GDP growth despite having a restrictive trade regime. The lessons of the Mauritian experience of "heterodox opening," however, are not clear, given the arguably unique configuration of internal and external factors that contributed to Mauritius' growth performance (Box 6.4). The replicability of the Mauritius model of export processing zones is also unclear given their limited success as a means of accelerating exports and growth in other countries (Box 6.5).

Box 6.2. Mozambique: Successful Trade Liberalization

Mozambique's trade liberalization began in the late 1980s and gathered momentum in the mid-1990s. The reforms undertaken—within the context of programs supported by the Enhanced Structural Adjustment Facility—involved the removal of quantitative import and export restrictions, the simplification of the tariff structure, the narrowing of tariff dispersion, the curtailment of exemptions, and the reduction of import and export taxes (see below). By the end of 1997, all significant non-tariff barriers had been eliminated, and only standard prohibitions relating to firearms and public health remained.

In 1996, the number of tariff rates was reduced from 12 to 5, and the average import-weighted tariff rate was lowered from 18.4 percent to 11 percent. A further reduction in the top tariff rate from 35 percent to 30 percent was implemented in April 1999. The current tariff structure is as follows: 0 percent on essential goods, 2.5 percent on raw materials, 5 percent on capital goods, 7.5 percent on intermediate goods, and 30 percent on consumer goods. Remaining distorting factors are generous exemptions under the investment law and import surcharges on cement, steel tubes, and sugar.

The government plans to reduce the top import tariff rate to 25 percent by January 2002. A ban on exports of raw cashews (Mozambique's second-largest export product) was replaced by a 40 percent export tax in 1995. The tax was subsequently reduced to 14 percent in 1996, although a new law was passed in October 1999 stipulating an increase to 18–22 percent. No other export taxes are in place.

Trade liberalization has been complemented by a comprehensive package of reforms undertaken during the last five years. These reforms comprised the development of a medium-term expenditure framework, a civil service reform, the rationalization of the tax system, the liberalization of interest rates, the introduction of interbank foreign exchange and money markets, and the privatization or restructuring of over 1,300 state-owned enterprises. The results obtained so far have been impressive: substantial investment has been channeled toward import substitution and nontraditional export activities, and the investment-to-GDP ratio rose from under 15 percent in the early 1990s to an average of 25 percent during 1997–99. Economic growth averaged 7 percent a year during 1993–95 and 10 percent a year during 1996–99, and inflation fell from over 50 percent in the early 1990s to single-digit levels in 1999.

Box 6.3. Zambia: Bold Liberalization but Low Growth

In the 1990s, Zambia implemented an ambitious macroeconomic stabilization and structural adjustment program, which included privatization, liberalization of the agricultural sector, and trade reform. Nevertheless, growth rates remained low owing to poor implementation of complementary policies and an unfavorable external environment. A major first step toward a more open trade system was taken in 1990 with a reduction in the maximum tariff from 100 percent to 50 percent. Following a phased reduction in nontariff barriers, most of the exchange restrictions on current international transactions were eliminated in 1994, and the dispersion of tariffs was further narrowed by raising the minimum rate to 20 percent while lowering the maximum rate from 50 percent to 40 percent. In 1995, there was some reversal of trade liberalization with the introduction, for fiscal reasons, of an across-the-board 5 percent import declaration fee (IDF). The effects of the IDF were, however, mitigated by the elimination of the 20 percent uplift factor applied to the sales tax in the same year. Further trade liberalization took place in 1996 when exemptions for government imports were abolished, and the average level of tariffs was brought down considerably through a 15 percent cut in most tariffs. The remaining nontariff barriers were removed in 1996 (except those kept for environmental, health, and security reasons), and the IDF was eliminated in 1998. Zambia now has a tariff regime with four rates, ranging from 0 to 25 percent, a statutory average rate of 14 percent, and specific rates on some products.

Despite some progress on macroeconomic stabilization, which was reflected in the reduction in fiscal deficits and inflation since the early 1990s, economic growth has remained subdued, mainly because of repeated droughts and delays in the privatization of the copper mines, which play a key role in the economy. Nonetheless, the liberalization effort has pushed the economy into a transformation process that has created favorable growth opportunities for a large number of enterprises—often newly established after 1993 or successfully restructured following privatization—as evidenced by the strong growth of nontraditional exports since the beginning of the decade. In 1992, metal exports—mainly copper and cobalt—constituted some 90 percent of total exports. However, reflecting generally weak copper prices and the falling productivity of the state-owned mining company, the total value of metal exports steadily declined in the following years from some US$1 billion in 1992 to only US$574 million in 1998. During the same period, nontraditional exports almost tripled, rising to US$288 million. The strongest growth, albeit from a low base, was recorded in floricultural and horticultural products, primary agricultural products, processed foods, engineering products, and textiles. As mentioned in Section V, Zambia was one of the few countries in sub-Saharan Africa that witnessed significant diversification of its exports.

Figure 6.1. Eastern and Southern Africa: Trade Liberalization and Economic Performance

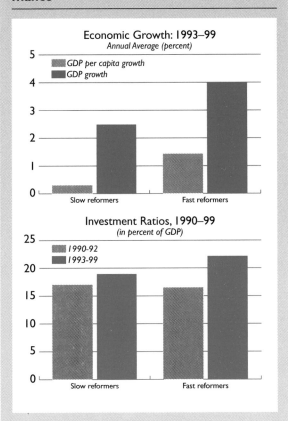

Economic Growth: 1993–99
Annual Average (percent)
■ GDP per capita growth
■ GDP growth
Slow reformers — Fast reformers

Investment Ratios, 1990–99
(in percent of GDP)
■ 1990-92
■ 1993-99
Slow reformers — Fast reformers

Figure 6.2. Eastern and Southern Africa: Trade Liberalization, Fiscal Performance, and External Balance
(Changes in percent of GDP)

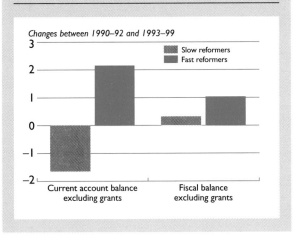

Changes between 1990–92 and 1993–99
■ Slow reformers
■ Fast reformers
Current account balance excluding grants — Fiscal balance excluding grants

Box 6.4. Mauritius: Heterodox Opening

At the beginning of the 1990s, Mauritius had a highly complicated trade regime, ridden with exemptions. There were 60 tariff bands, the top rate was about 600 percent, and the average tariff rate was about 80 percent. Some liberalization was implemented during the 1990s, beginning with the reduction of quantitative restrictions in 1991. By 1994, the number of non-zero rate bands was reduced to 7, and the maximum tariff rate was lowered to 80 percent. The export duty on sugar and all controls on exports were also eliminated, except for some items that still require export permits or prior approvals (for example, tea, spices, and pharmaceuticals). In July 1998, however, an additional rate band of 10 percent was added. There are also additional import excise levies ranging from 15 to 400 percent. In 1998, the average tariff was about 19 percent.

Despite these reforms, Mauritius' import regime remains restrictive (with a restrictiveness rating of 7 out of 10), as reflected in its still substantial QRs, high and dispersed tariff rates, and complexity. Another significant feature of the trade regime is the high level of unclassified exemptions, exemptions to the EPZ and other investment incentive schemes, and concessions by ministries. The restrictiveness of the import regime has not translated in a tax on the two major export products—sugar and textiles—which have been sheltered from the effects of import protection through the export processing zones and by government measures that until recently prevented spillovers of wage pressures from the importable to exportable sector. In addition, preferential quotas in export markets for sugar and textiles have ensured high returns (and rents) to exportables that have helped finance higher investment levels. It remains to be seen whether such a strategy will be sustainable in a changing external environment where rents from export quotas begin to decline and where domestic wage spillovers become increasingly difficult to prevent.

Fiscal Aspects of Trade Liberalization

A recent study (Ebrill, Stotsky, and Gropp, 1999) examines the theory and experience of the revenue implications of trade reform. On the theoretical side, some important conclusions can be drawn. First, revenue is less likely to be affected by trade reform when the initial position is highly restrictive; when trade liberalization involves the tariffication and/or elimination of quotas, and elimination of exemptions, simplification, and reduction of tariff dispersion; when there are simultaneous re-

Box 6.5. Export Processing Zones

In early 1998, the following ESA countries had in place legislation for export processing zones (EPZs): Botswana, Kenya, Madagascar, Mauritius, Mozambique, Namibia, Uganda, and Tanzania (Madani, 1999). Although the features of the various EPZs in the region differ from country to country, most of them have some key elements in common: (i) generous corporate income tax exemptions, with tax holidays of up to 10 years and concessional tax rates afterward; (ii) duty-free access to inputs and capital goods; and (iii) relaxed labor laws. In some countries, export processing firms that are not located in designated geographical areas are also eligible for the incentives. Despite their appeal, however, EPZs have major disadvantages, including potentially large tax revenue losses and leakages, distortive impact on the competitiveness of domestic firms that do not benefit from the incentives, and ample scope for abuses. As a result, their overall success in the ESA region and in sub-Sa-

haran Africa in general has been rather limited. The anticipated gains in foreign direct investment, production, and employment in EPZs have not materialized in most countries, with the exception of Mauritius, where the establishment of an EPZ in 1971 contributed to a substantial increase in exports of clothing and textiles. In addition, the development of EPZs in most ESA countries has been negatively affected by implementation problems (notably weak and/or nontransparent administration) and the slow progress in some of the key areas of adjustment, including macroeconomic stabilization and infrastructure development. The experience of these countries underscores the view that sound economic policies, coupled with a strong structural adjustment effort (including trade liberalization) are a first-best policy, and that special tax incentives may not be able to offset the negative impact of an unfavorable and unstable policy environment.

Table 6.1. Selected ESA Countries: Tariff Revenue
(Percent of GDP)

Country	1980	1985	1990	Last Available Year[1]
Botswana	13.22	8.16	6.60	5.85
Burundi[3]	3.74	2.37	...	2.51
Congo, Dem. Rep. of[3]	1.94	3.17	3.26	1.33
Ethiopia	2.76	2.78	2.19	2.30
Kenya	3.89	3.28	3.83	3.94
Lesotho	...	29.26	21.95	32.27
Malawi[3]	4.09	3.70	3.05	3.02
Mauritius[3]	7.50	9.48	10.21	6.74
Rwanda	2.98	...	2.17	3.22
South Africa	0.72	0.73	0.98	0.18
Zambia	2.07	2.86	3.53	3.06
Zimbabwe	1.06	4.57	5.20	4.30
Average (Sub-Saharan Africa)[2]	4.82	5.81	5.20	5.39
Average (Eastern and Southern Africa)	4.00	6.40	5.72	5.73
Non-OECD Asia and Pacific[2,4]	3.15	3.53	4.16	3.42
Middle East[2]	4.18	3.95	3.27	3.48
Non-OECD Western Hemisphere[2]	2.78	2.51	2.43	2.36
OECD[2,5]	0.87	0.75	0.58	0.37

Sources: IMF, *Government Finance Statistics*, various issues, and *World Economic Outlook* (October 1997); and OECD, *Revenue Statistics*, various issues, except as noted.

[1]Last year for which data are available is 1996.

[2]Data are unweighted averages.

[3]Data provided by the country authorities; and IMF staff estimates.

[4]Korea joined the OECD in December 1996.

[5]Excluding the Czech Republic, Hungary, Luxembourg, and Poland. The OECD data for the countries of the European Union (EU) are for tariff collections at the borders of those countries and accordingly differ from the tariff collections on goods used in each EU country to the extent that there is transshipment within the union.

forms of customs and tax administration; and when trade liberalization is supported by macroeconomic policies that maintain external balance and avoid a concomitant real appreciation of the liberalizing country's currency. Second, beyond a certain point, and even allowing for the above factors, a reduction of tariffs will lead to a decline in the importance of trade tax revenue, highlighting the need for domestic tax reform to enhance the domestic tax base.

What has been the experience of the ESA countries that have undertaken significant trade and tariff liberalization? Three facts stand out:

- First, at the start of the reforms, ESA countries (with the exception of SACU countries)[28] depended to a great extent on trade taxes for their total revenues. In 1990, the trade tax revenue-to-GDP ratio of ESA countries was 5.7 percent, significantly higher than that for other groups of developing countries (Table 6.1). On average, the slow reformers were considerably more dependent on trade taxes than the fast reformers (Table 6.2). This dependence on trade taxes may have conditioned the nature and extent of trade liberalization. In the case of South Africa, fiscal considerations did not play a significant role in the decision to liberalize trade because of the country's limited dependence on customs duties for revenue generation (customs duties accounted for just about 4 percent of total revenue, of which a substantial part was transferred to BLNS countries under existing revenue-sharing arrangements). In the case of Malawi, trade liberalization in the mid-1990s was reversed because of a deteriorating fiscal situation, which, in turn, led to the imposition of an export tax. Similarly, in Tanzania, extensive leakages stemming from weak administration and rampant exemptions led to a slowdown of trade liberalization and efforts to address the tax policy and tax administration problems.

- Second, there was a substantial reduction in the reliance on trade taxes during the course of the 1990s. On average, trade taxes decreased from 34 percent to 23 percent of total revenue, with a broadly similar rate of decrease in both fast and slow reformers. But total tax revenue-to-GDP ratios remained rather stable during the 1990s, reflecting efforts by ESA countries to reform their domestic tax system and broaden the base of trade-neutral taxes. The impact of

---

[28]The BLNS countries are excluded from the analysis here because their "trade taxes" largely represent transfers from South Africa under the revenue-sharing arrangements in SACU.

Table 6.2. Eastern and Southern Africa: Trade Tax Revenue as a Share of Total Revenue[1]
(Percent)

	1991/92	1997/98
Moderate or no liberalization		
Angola	...	5
Burundi	36	29
Comoros	68	55
Ethiopia	...	26
Kenya	...	15
Madagascar	41	29
Mauritius	44	34
Rwanda	34	24
Seychelles	53	26
Tanzania	22	29
Zimbabwe	18	17
Average	40	26
Substantial liberalization		
Botswana	...	14
Lesotho	...	...
Malawi	...	21
Namibia	...	28
South Africa	8	4
Swaziland	...	50
Mozambique	26	18
Uganda	42	12
Zambia	20	16
Average	24	14

Sources: IMF, African Department database, and *World Economic Outlook* database.

[1]The averages exclude Botswana, Lesotho, Namibia, and Swaziland.

---

fiscal reform has varied within the ESA countries. In the case of Tanzania, dependence on revenue from trade taxes increased, partly as a result of efforts in the latter part of the 1990s to strengthen customs administration; the outcome, however, also reflected a more modest effort of tariff liberalization. In Zambia, although tariff reform proceeded at a rapid pace, reliance on trade taxes did not diminish substantially because there was a concomitant effort to tackle the problem of pervasive exemptions.

- Third, on average, trade liberalization is associated with an improvement in the overall fiscal position in 1993–99 (Figure 6.2). Two-thirds of the countries in the substantial liberalization group had improved their fiscal balance since the early 1990s, despite a reduced reliance on trade taxes, pointing to the success of offsetting tax and expenditure measures that were part of broader programs of fiscal consolidation.

VII   Trade Policy Issues Ahead

In coming years, ESA countries will be affected by the ongoing trend of trade liberalization at the regional level (Table 7.1). The EU-South Africa free trade agreement (EU-SA FTA) will also have significant trade and competitiveness effects for ESA countries with strong trade links with both the EU and South Africa; it will also have important revenue effects for several countries, notably the BLNS countries (Box 7.1). More fundamentally, it will impel a lowering of trade barriers in ESA countries, in part because their borders are porous. Direct pressures to lower trade barriers will also arise in the context of discussions about the trade arrangements that will succeed the Lomé Convention.

Each of these developments raises a set of important issues, namely, the unfinished agenda on unilateral liberalization, preferential integration within the region, preferential integration with industrial country partners, multilateral liberalization and the next round of trade negotiations in the WTO, the role of complementary policies, and the role of trading partners.

The Unfinished Agenda of Unilateral Liberalization

As discussed, many ESA countries made substantial progress on trade liberalization during the 1990s, but a large unfinished agenda lies ahead. First, 9 out of the group of 22 ESA countries, including Ethiopia, Kenya, and Zimbabwe, still have restrictive regimes, with pervasive quantitative restrictions and high tariffs, often in excess of 25 percent. Second, even in countries that have liberalized their trade regimes substantially, a number of problems relating to complexity and exemptions remain. South Africa is an example of a country with an overly complex tariff system, with 72 tariff lines and a high proportion of non–ad valorem tariffs. Mozambique protects its sugar and cashew industries with highly distortive trade taxes, subsidizing firms of doubtful viability. Furthermore, collection efficiency in ESA countries is very poor (often less than 50 percent), reflecting, among other things, the

continuing problems that arise from generous exemptions. In Mauritius, for instance, forgone revenues from exemptions amount to about 75 percent of collections, and about 50 percent of collections when exemptions for exports are excluded.

Regional Preferential Integration

Many of the current RTAs in the region do not seem to possess the characteristics of a natural trading bloc in the sense of their products being usefully complementary. This is particularly the case of COMESA, where countries trade less with each other than what would be expected on the basis of their levels of economic development and geographical proximity (Subramanian and Tamirisa, 2000). This reinforces the principle that preferential trade arrangements in the ESA region should be outward-oriented and pursue MFN liberalization with as much vigor as intraregional liberalization. The CBI has embodied the principle of open regionalism, and COMESA is moving in that direction too. In the case of SADC, average external tariffs are lower than for CBI and COMESA countries, but reform needs to be extended to those selected labor-intensive products where restrictions remain high.

ESA is, perhaps uniquely, distinguished by the proliferation of a number of overlapping and eventually inconsistent regional arrangements (see Figure 7.1). This is in contrast to Asia and Latin America, where RTAs have less overlap and, hence, limited scope for conflict. Several problems arise as a result of such proliferation. First, some countries that are currently members of a customs union (Namibia and Swaziland) cannot offer different preferences to other groups of countries. This problem will be compounded if COMESA implements its common external tariff in 2004 as planned. There are also complications for the SADC countries that are members of COMESA, as it is not clear whether they would follow COMESA or SADC rules. Second, when countries are simultaneously members of several RTAs, implementation of the agreements can be difficult, as incentives for inefficient diversion of trade through

Table 7.1. Eastern and Southern Africa: Changes in the Trading Environment[1]

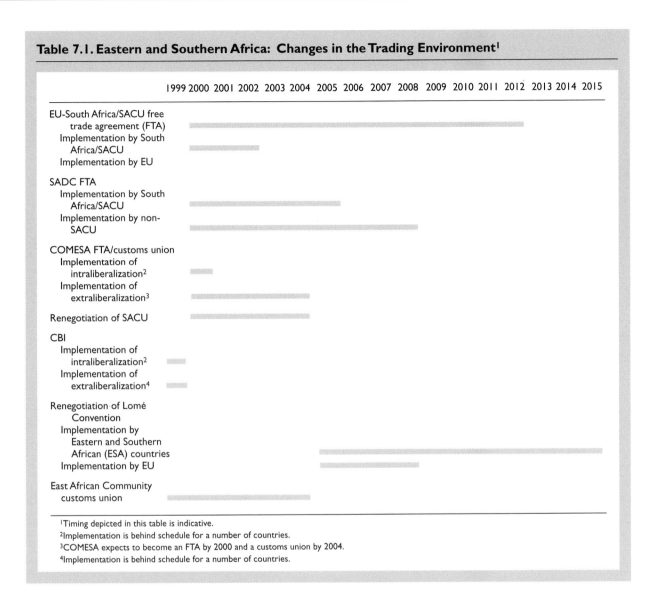

	1999	2000	2001	2002	2003	2004	2005	2006	2007	2008	2009	2010	2011	2012	2013	2014	2015

EU-South Africa/SACU free trade agreement (FTA)
   Implementation by South Africa/SACU
   Implementation by EU

SADC FTA
   Implementation by South Africa/SACU
   Implementation by non-SACU

COMESA FTA/customs union
   Implementation of intraliberalization[2]
   Implementation of extraliberalization[3]

Renegotiation of SACU

CBI
   Implementation of intraliberalization[2]
   Implementation of extraliberalization[4]

Renegotiation of Lomé Convention
   Implementation by Eastern and Southern African (ESA) countries
   Implementation by EU

East African Community customs union

[1]Timing depicted in this table is indicative.
[2]Implementation is behind schedule for a number of countries.
[3]COMESA expects to become an FTA by 2000 and a customs union by 2004.
[4]Implementation is behind schedule for a number of countries.

areas with lower external tariffs or less onerous internal procedures emerge and customs officials are faced with the task of establishing the origin of goods coming from different groups of countries. In fact, ESA countries might find rules of origin impossible to implement, particularly if they differ among countries. Rules of origin will also complicate marketing and production decisions, as well as the rationalization of production (companies will have an incentive to differentiate between production for the region with local inputs and for the rest of the world with cheaper inputs). Third, the sheer administrative and political costs and distraction stemming from multiple initiatives create difficulties. Therefore, there is an urgent need to rationalize these initiatives in order to improve the chances for their success and the investment climate in the region.

One suggestion to encourage wider regional cooperation and liberalization is to establish a forum comprising all ESA countries and to take a closer look at the costs of these multiple initiatives. The essential requirement is not necessarily to combine the different RTAs into one, but at least to ensure that their policies are designed and implemented in a mutually consistent fashion. In any case, it would be helpful if all the RTAs were to adopt similar and low external tariffs.

Is There a Need for Compensation?

A widely held view among ESA countries is that regional integration would entail the need for compensation, particularly when one of the partners is economically dominant. While this argument may

Box 7.1. The Impact of Changes in the Trade Environment on the BLNS Countries

Important developments in the trade environment are expected to have an impact on Botswana, Lesotho, Namibia, and Swaziland (the BLNS countries), which, along with South Africa, constitute the South African Customs Union (SACU). The EU-South Africa free trade agreement or FTA, the renegotiation of the revenue-sharing arrangements among SACU countries, the post-Lomé Convention arrangements, the SADC FTA (to a lesser extent), and the future multilateral trade round under the auspices of the WTO are expected to have the following effects:

- An *adverse competitiveness* impact, as the EU-SA FTA will reduce many of the preferential margins that BLNS suppliers enjoy vis-à-vis the EU under the Lomé Convention. This FTA and the SADC FTA will also erode BLNS suppliers' margin in the South African market relative to EU suppliers and non-SACU SADC suppliers. This could result not only in lost trade but also in investment diversion away from BLNS countries, as the erosion of preferential margins makes them a less attractive source of supply.

- A *beneficial pull* effect will be felt from the growth impulse imparted to South Africa as a result of these developments.

- An *adverse impact* on revenue transfers to the BLNS countries will result from a combination of reduced *total receipts* (as tariffs decline under the EU-SA FTA, SADC, and the next WTO round) and

reduced shares stemming from the SACU renegotiations (for any given aggregate pool).

The competitiveness impact is likely to be limited since BLNS exports do not compete directly with EU or South African products. According to a detailed study (IDS/BIDPA, 1998), the value of BLNS products threatened by direct competition is relatively small; the quantitative impact will depend on how these products are treated in the EU-SA FTA and in the post-Lomé arrangements. The pull exerted on BLNS countries as a result of higher growth in South Africa—estimated at about 1 percent—is difficult to quantify. While small, it could nevertheless offset any adverse competitiveness impact in the BLNS countries.

The revenue effect, which is probably the most significant one, is summarized in the table below.

With respect to the revenue impact, three points are noteworthy. First, the trade developments are expected to affect Lesotho and Swaziland most, as they depend more on SACU revenues than Namibia and Botswana. Second, the full revenue impact will be seen only by the year 2010 when the EU-SA FTA will be fully implemented. Third, the magnitude of impact is subject to considerable uncertainty, depending on several factors, including the new revenue-sharing arrangement under SACU, the exemptions under the EU-SA FTA, and the new WTO round. For these countries, the policy implications are clear: efforts to enhance the domestic tax base, especially for Lesotho and Swaziland, are imperative if the adverse revenue effects arising from changes in the trading environment are to be offset.

	Botswana	Lesotho	Namibia	Swaziland
SACU revenues (percent of total revenues)[1]	15.3	48.1	27.7	50.0
SACU revenues (percent of GDP)[1]	5.5	23.6	10.1	15.6
Reduction in SACU revenues[2]	−5 to −9	−13 to −21	−9 to −14	−14 to −28
Value of Lomé preferences (millions of rand)[3]	9.9	0.2	6.1	20.0

[1] In 1998/99.
[2] In percent (IDS and BIDPA, 1998).
[3] Imani (1997).

hold in principle, the case for compensation that would be directed at South Africa would be conditioned to a large extent on how open the South African market becomes, particularly in the labor-intensive sectors in which partner countries have a comparative advantage (for example, clothing and textiles). Opening these sectors would engender the

perception that partner countries could gain from the agreement and, hence, mute calls for other forms of compensation (transfers). Although the principle of asymmetric liberalization in the SADC is a form of transitional compensation, it will only have the desired effect if it eventually encompasses all the sectors that are of particular importance to South

Africa's regional trading partners, including those that are currently highly protected. In the case of the Common Market of the South (MERCOSUR) and North American Free Trade Agreement (NAFTA), the question of compensation never arose because of the perception that the smaller countries stood to gain from the liberalization unleashed by the agreements. In sum, as long as the regional integration scheme is appropriately designed, a compensation arrangement should not be necessary.

Liberalization of Investment and Services

As noted before, preferential integration for ESA countries in the area of trade in goods may not be the best approach to reap the benefits of globalization. A similar conclusion can be drawn when looking at trade in services and investment liberalization, because the most efficient service providers are likely to be in the industrial countries. This does not preclude greater cooperation in services and investment among ESA countries. One possible area of cooperation would be domestic regulation in the various services sectors, where ESA countries could pool resources and aim to achieve convergence in domestic regulatory regimes. This objective is already being pursued in the context of the financial sector and could be extended to sectors such as telecommunications, power, and transport. In the limit, there could even be common regulators for ESA countries in all these areas.

Preferential Agreements with Industrial Countries

Two important imminent developments for the region are the EU-SA FTA and the renegotiation of the Lomé Convention. Since the share of non-EU countries in the trade of ESA countries is about 55 percent, there is considerable scope for inefficient trade diversion consequent upon the FTA. Unlike integration within the region, integration with the EU will have important revenue consequences, and if the efficiency gains are not forthcoming, ESA countries could be seriously disadvantaged. To counter these risks, ESA countries should continue to reduce their MFN tariffs while strengthening the domestic sources of tax revenue. Given the timetables for these agreements, their impact is likely to be felt only toward the end of this decade. This provides ESA countries with an opportunity to adjust to these developments.

Multilateral Liberalization

Sub-Saharan African countries did not, in general, take advantage of the Uruguay Round in ad-

vancing their own liberalization (Harrold, 1995; and Wang and Winters, 1998) and failed to use the WTO as a mechanism to lock in the reforms that were already under way. As described above, this was true in the area of both trade in goods and trade in services, as reflected in the large wedge between actual trade regimes and the regimes that were bound under the WTO. It must be recognized that in a mercantilist framework, such as the one underlying the WTO, ESA countries are disadvantaged to some extent. By virtue of their small markets, they have little to offer to their trading partners and, therefore, face little pressure from them to undertake trade liberalization.

In any new round of multilateral trade negotiations, ESA countries should at least use the WTO as a binding mechanism to lock in any reforms they undertake. In view of the history of reversals, including during the 1990s, and the attendant loss in policy credibility, it would be especially important to find a credible anchor for trade and other policies. This would apply not only to trade in goods, but also to trade in services. Developing countries have recently used the WTO services negotiations to lock in future regimes and to strengthen domestic regulations that can then facilitate further liberalization of key services sectors (Mattoo, 1999). ESA countries could also emulate this approach for trade in services.

The Further Decline of Preferences

One of the likely outcomes of the next round of multilateral trade negotiations will be the further erosion of preferential margins enjoyed by ESA countries. They will thus need to adjust to a trading environment in which reliance on preferences cannot be a basis for integration with the world economy. This erosion will stem from different sources, including further declines in industrial country tariffs on industrial products. For ESA countries, the elimination of the multifiber arrangement (the system of preferential access in textiles and clothing) and any further liberalization of the agricultural sector in OECD countries will make the biggest dent in their preferential benefits. The liberalization of agriculture and dismantling of the multifiber arrangement, by reducing world prices, will erode the rents they currently enjoy as a result of preferential quotas. For countries such as Mauritius, the loss of preferential access may have a significant impact on their growth strategy, and adjustment to the new environment acquires real significance. Similarly, the BLNS countries, which have guaranteed quotas in beef and sugar, will face declining export revenues.

Figure 7.1. Main Regional Trade Arrangements

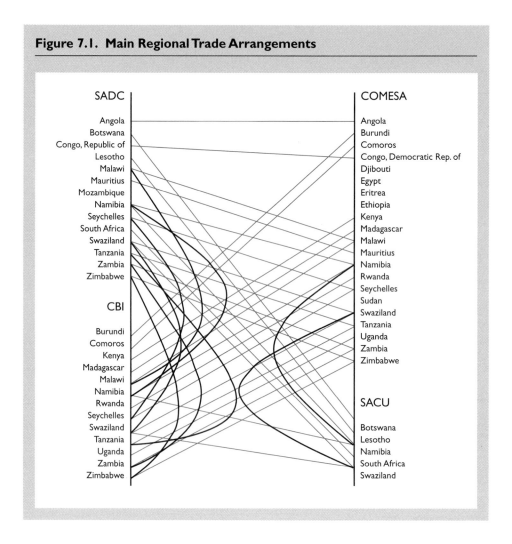

Role of Complementary Policies

The Need for Fiscal Adjustment

Whether the cause is further unilateral liberalization or the implementation of regional agreements within Africa and with the EU, trade taxes will represent a steadily declining source of revenue for ESA countries in the coming years. Moreover, the magnitudes of this decline could be substantial. As the experience in the 1990s has shown, however, the phasing in of tariff reductions over a number of years leaves sufficient time for the countries in the region to adjust to the imminent changes. ESA countries need to strengthen further domestic sources of revenue—through a broadening of the revenue base, the introduction of new taxes where appropriate, and a strengthening of tax administration. Much of the improvements in the tax systems will need to come from the rationalization of exemptions and generous investment incentives. It is far from clear that these

incentives really augment the total flow of investment to the region, and there is scope for cooperation among ESA countries to avoid wasteful tax competition for investment. This could mean an emphasis on greater convergence of tax regimes and on cost-effective, transparent, and well-administered incentives.

The Need for Complementary Domestic Policies

The individual case studies of trade reform reported in this paper point to the need for complementary domestic policies, in order to allow reforms to be implemented and sustained, and to unleash the favorable supply responses expected from increased integration. The determinants of growth are complex and include a number of policy, institutional, geographical, and exogenous variables (political developments, terms of trade, etc.). But experience shows that policies aimed at maintaining macroeconomic stability, removing structural bottlenecks, and creating an open and liberal investment regime are required to promote rapid and sustainable economic growth.

Role of Major Trading Partners

Achieving integration in the world economy is predominantly determined by domestic policy actions, although a favorable external trading environment can also play a supportive role. What can ESA countries' major trading partners do to foster such an environment? The first-best approach would be the elimination of all industrial countries' market access barriers on African exports on a MFN basis, combined with unilateral, nondiscriminatory trade liberalization by African countries. A second approach would be for the main industrial countries to enter into reciprocal free trade agreements with ESA countries. Under this approach, ESA countries would suffer relatively little trade diversion from such comprehensive agreements because nearly all their major suppliers (the United States, EU, Canada, and Japan) would be included. A third approach would be for the industrial countries to eliminate on an MFN and nonreciprocal basis all market access barriers on products of export interest to African countries and to bind these in the WTO (Wang and Winters, 1998). Another possibility would be for trading partners to reduce market access barriers to African exports on a preferential and nonreciprocal basis and bind these also in the WTO.[29] It is far from clear that this approach, involving a continuation and extension of existing nonreciprocal preferential arrangements, such as the Lomé Convention, would be beneficial. The African experience (under the Lomé Convention and Generalized System of Preferences) demonstrates that preferences have not led to successful integration and may actually have encouraged inefficient specialization.

Specific Actions

The first two approaches discussed above would be preferable but difficult to achieve in the near future. The third one would be nondiscriminatory and, hence, consistent with WTO rules, but its quantitative impact would be uncertain, given that MFN tariffs on African exports are generally low. There are, however, some specific actions industrial countries might undertake in the short run to promote the integration of African countries into the world economy.

- MFN bound and applied tariffs on agricultural goods of interest to ESA countries could be eliminated, market access commitments could be implemented transparently, and exemption from special safeguards measures could be granted. Particular attention should be paid to tariff peaks and also to tariffs on processed goods, so that tariff escalation might be reduced (on wood and leather products, for example). If, as a second best, access is granted to ESA countries preferentially, both new and existing preferences should be tariff free, unconditional, and free of ceiling quotas. In addition, market access would be improved if industrial countries simplified their rules of origin requirements.

- The phasing in of Uruguay Round liberalization on products of export interest to Africa could be accelerated. Tariff cuts on textiles and garments and the abolition of quotas and special safeguards for these products, for example, will encourage exports and, if offered preferentially, assist the ESA countries to gain market experience before the multifiber arrangement is phased out and a much more competitive environment is ushered in.

- More generally, tariff escalation should be reduced by extending tariff cuts to all stages of production to remove obstacles to the processing of primary commodities and to encourage export diversification.[30] Even though when preferences are taken into account sub-Saharan African countries face low average tariffs in industrial countries,[31] these low tariffs do not extend to processed and temperate agricultural products or to textiles and garments. Outside the Lomé Convention, African countries face the same high tariffs and nontariff barrier regimes as the industrial countries' other non-FTA partners, even though their low level of industrialization means that their exports attain neither the level nor the

---

[29]The African Growth and Opportunity Act, enacted by the U.S. Congress in early 2000, provides for duty-free treatment of the exports of sub-Saharan African countries to the United States. The magnitude of benefits to these countries, especially in relation to textiles and clothing products, will be determined by rules of origin requirements that need to be fulfilled to qualify for duty-free access. An interesting feature of the Act is that it envisages the possible negotiation of free trade agreements between the United States and African countries in the future.

[30]Tariff escalation is significant for many product chains relevant to sub-Saharan African countries, such as wood products, textiles and clothing, fish, and leather products (Amjadi, Reinke, and Yeats, 1996).

[31]Pre-Uruguay Round tariffs facing sub-Saharan African countries' exports to the EU, United States, and Japan averaged only 0.31 percent, less than for any other group of developing countries (Amjadi, Reinke, and Yeats, 1996).

composition necessary to threaten sectors in industrial countries.

• Although the Uruguay Round agreements allow contingent protection actions in particular circumstances, the industrial countries could exempt African countries from antidumping, countervailing, and safeguard actions. Starting from very low bases, African exports can sometimes record very rapid growth rates and be hard hit by contingent protection measures. The absolute volumes of African exports are, however, not large enough to be a threat to industrialized countries, even if they approach the thresholds set out in the Uruguay Round agreements.

This discussion of the main trade policy issues facing ESA countries leads to the following conclusions. First, for a number of ESA countries, particularly those with restricted trade regimes, there is an urgent need to push ahead with unilateral liberalization so that the benefits of reduced rent-seeking activities, increased efficiency, and improved export performance can be reaped. Second, liberalization should extend beyond trade in goods to cover services and investment regimes. Third, in any new round of multilateral trade negotiations, ESA countries should use the WTO to lock in any reforms they undertake and reap the attendant benefits of signaling the durability of reform efforts. Fourth, there is a need to rationalize the multiplicity of regional initiatives and to embrace the principle of open regionalism by reducing barriers to trade with all countries, thereby minimizing the risks associated with preferential integration. Fifth, industrial countries should assist the trade liberalization efforts of ESA countries by reducing market access barriers and eliminating restrictions on African exports. An attractive option in this regard would be for the major industrial countries to negotiate reciprocal free trade agreements with ESA countries. This would improve market access for ESA countries while also furthering their own liberalization efforts. Lastly, it is important to emphasize that the success of these efforts will depend critically on a comprehensive set of complementary domestic policies aimed at ensuring macroeconomic stability, strengthening domestic institutions, and providing a more secure and predictable environment for investment.

Appendix I Overall Trade Restrictiveness Classification Scheme

As noted in Sharer and others (1998), the restrictiveness of the tariff regime depends on many factors, including the minimum and maximum tariff rates, the number of bands, the allocation of individual items to the bands, the existence of "exceptional" rates that lie outside the basic tariff structure, any other duties and charges (such as differential rates of excise or value-added taxes on imports, import surcharges, and statistical fees), and the extent of exemptions from customs duties. The classification scheme for overall trade restrictiveness used in this study builds on the approach developed by Sharer and others by including information on export taxes and by adding another category of nontariff barrier (NTB) restrictiveness.

Under this approach, a country is assigned a restrictiveness ranking for both its price-based (import tariffs and export taxes) measures and its NTBs, based on the classification schemes described below. Consistent with the Lerner theorem that an export tax is equivalent to an import tax, the price-based measure is computed as the sum of import and export taxes. Whenever possible, an unweighted average of statutory tariff rates including other duties and charges was used. An average of statutory tariff rates is preferable to one based on customs collections since the latter reflects (often extensive) exemptions. An unweighted average is preferable to a trade-weighted average since items with high tariffs are likely to have small trade weights. Other duties and charges should also be included. The restrictiveness ranking accords greater weight to NTBs, which are inherently less transparent and more distortionary than tariffs.

NTBs include quantitative restrictions, restructure licensing, bans, state trading monopolies, restrictive foreign exchange practices that affect the trade regime (for example, a surrender requirement at a nonmarket exchange rate, multiple exchange rates), quality controls, and customs procedures that act as trade restrictions. Such measures in effect provide indirect subsidies to import-competing domestic producers in a nontransparent manner. However, information on NTBs and their restrictiveness as measured, for instance, by ad valorem

| Trade Taxes[2] | Absolutely No Restrictions | Nontariff Barriers[1] | | Pervasive Restrictions; Greater than 40 Percent Coverage[3] |
		Few Restrictions; 0–20 Percent Coverage[3]	Substantial Restrictions; 20–40 Percent Coverage[3]	
<10 percent	1	3	5	7
10 to 15 percent	2	4	6	8
15 to 20 percent	3	5	7	9
20 to 25 percent	4	6	8	10
25 to 35 percent	5	7	9	10
>35 percent	10	10	10	10

[1]Includes restrictions on exports and imports and other NTBs.
[2]Includes customs duties and all other charges levied exclusively on imports, as well as export taxes.
[3]Refers to the share of total trade being affected by NTBs.

equivalents,[1] may either not be available for all countries or be of limited use.[2] A review of previous studies on trade reform in developing countries below shows that other researchers have faced similar difficulties. In view of this, this study utilizes four categories of NTBs (see table above).

The table illustrates the assignment of price-based and NTB categories on the 10-point scale. A country is assigned an overall rating of 10 as long as the average tariff rate exceeds 35 percent, even if the nontariff trade regime is classified as open. Countries with an overall rating of between 7 and 10 are classified as restrictive; those with a 5 or a 6 rating are classified as moderately restrictive; those with 3 or 4 as moderately open; and those with 1 or 2 as open.

---

[1]The ad valorem equivalent of an import quota is the rate of ad valorem tariff that would yield the same import quantity as the quota. There are many circumstances in which import quotas and import tariffs are not equivalent, including imperfect market structures and changes in supply and demand.

[2]Trade or production coverage of NTBs may be useful but does not fully capture their restrictiveness.

Appendix II   Statistical Tables

Table A1. Eastern and Southern Africa: Structure of Production (Constant Prices), 1985–97[1]

	Agriculture			Industry			Services		
	1985	1990	1997	1985	1990	1997	1985	1990	1997
Angola	14.0	12.2	8.2	50.2	54.1	68.0	35.4	33.9	26.0
Botswana[2]	5.6	5.5	4.6	68.1	54.5	50.6	43.0	45.1	55.8
Burundi	50.2	48.8	51.2	22.7	22.7	17.3	28.2	29.9	30.2
Comoros	38.3	42.2	44.5	15.7	9.6	14.6	57.3	57.5	55.1
Congo, Dem. Rep. of	30.0	32.7	61.8	35.7	27.6	17.4	43.7	43.1	21.7
Eritrea	...	...	...	...	...	...	...	...	...
Ethiopia	...	...	...	...	...	...	...	...	...
Kenya	35.7	34.4	30.7	16.3	16.4	15.7	48.5	49.5	53.5
Lesotho	23.5	20.7	12.3	23.7	30.9	39.1	57.7	51.2	48.6
Madagascar	30.6	31.2	32.4	14.0	13.6	13.7	55.9	55.6	54.0
Malawi	29.4	26.7	36.3	19.3	20.9	17.5	51.8	53.9	43.7
Mauritius	17.6	12.8	9.4	27.8	32.9	33.1	55.3	54.7	57.5
Mozambique	33.5	26.3	30.2	39.0	19.5	26.4	27.5	54.1	43.4
Namibia	10.0	12.0	11.3	33.6	31.2	32.1	56.1	57.2	56.8
Rwanda	43.1	39.6	36.4	24.0	22.6	24.2	32.9	37.8	39.4
Seychelles[3]	...	8.0	5.0	...	21.5	35.4	...	102.1	88.0
South Africa	4.5	5.0	5.3	41.9	40.3	38.7	53.2	54.5	56.0
Swaziland	32.0	22.5	17.1	23.7	41.2	43.5	51.6	38.9	39.9
Tanzania[4]	44.3	44.3	46.6	22.6	22.9	21.4	33.4	33.2	31.9
Uganda	57.8	56.4	46.0	10.0	11.3	16.9	33.0	32.9	36.8
Zambia	22.9	24.0	16.0	46.1	49.3	35.6	43.2	39.8	62.1
Zimbabwe	18.7	16.1	16.6	33.1	34.3	28.1	48.4	49.8	55.3
Eastern and Southern Africa (weighted)	11.1	12.2	13.1	38.1	36.0	35.5	49.5	49.7	52.1
Eastern and Southern Africa (unweighted)	28.5	26.1	26.1	29.9	28.9	29.5	45.1	48.7	47.8
Sub-Saharan Africa	18.4	19.2	20.1	37.0	35.7	33.8	47.1	47.0	47.4
Middle Income[5]	n.a.	12.9	13.2	...	38.0	41.9	...	50.6	54.3

Source: World Bank, *World Development Indicators*, 1999.

[1]Ratio of appropriate sectoral variable to GDP at factor cost. All averages are unweighted unless indicated otherwise. In a few cases, shares do not add up to 100.

[2]Final period refers to 1995.

[3]Initial period refers to 1988.

[4]Initial period refers to 1988 and final period to 1996.

[5]Initial period refers to 1988.

Table A2. Eastern and Southern Africa: Countries with IMF Arrangements During the 1990s

	1990	1991	1992	1993	1994	1995	1996	1997	1998	1999
Angola										
Botswana										
Burundi		•	•	•	•					
Comoros		•	•	•	•					
Congo, Dem. Rep. of	•						•	•	•	•
Eritrea										
Ethiopia			•	•	•	•	•	•	•	•
Kenya	•	•	•	•	•		•	•	•	•
Lesotho	•	•	•	•	•		•	•		
Madagascar	•	•	•				•	•	•	•
Malawi	•	•	•	•	•	•	•	•	•	•
Mauritius										
Mozambique	•	•	•	•	•	•	•	•	•	•
Namibia										
Rwanda		•	•	•	•				•	•
Seychelles										
South Africa										
Swaziland										
Tanzania	•	•	•	•	•		•	•	•	•
Uganda	•	•	•	•	•	•	•	•	•	•
Zambia						•	•	•	•	
Zimbabwe			•	•	•	•			•	•

Source: IMF, *International Financial Statistics.*

Table A3. Sachs-Warner Classification of Trade Policy of ESA Countries, 1980s and 1990s

	1980s Overall	Late 1990s[1] Overall
Angola	Open	Closed
Botswana	. . .	Open
Burundi	Closed	Closed
Comoros	. . .	Closed
Congo, Dem. Rep. of	Closed	Open
Ethiopia	Closed	Open
Kenya	Closed	Open
Lesotho	. . .	Open
Madagascar	. . .	Open
Malawi	Closed	Open
Mauritius	Open	Open
Mozambique	Closed	Open
Namibia	. . .	Open
Rwanda	Closed	Open
Seychelles	. . .	Closed
South Africa	Closed	Open
Swaziland	. . .	Open
Tanzania	Closed	Open
Uganda	Closed	Open
Zambia	Closed	Open
Zimbabwe	Closed	Closed
No. of "open" countries in ESA	2	17
Total countries in ESA	14	21
No. of "open" countries in SSA	7	18
Total countries in SSA	25	25
No. of "open" countries in Asia	7	11
Total countries in Asia	15	15
No. of "open" countries in Middle East and North Africa	2	1
Total countries in Middle East and North Africa	9	9
No. of "open" countries in W. Hemisphere	3	22
Total countries in Western Hemisphere	22	22
No. of "open" industrial countries	22	24
Total industrial countries	24	24

[1]IMF staff's calculations applying the Sachs-Warner criterion for tariffs and nontariff barriers. That is, a country is classified as closed if its NTBs covered 40 percent or more of the value of trade or if its average tariff exceeded 40 percent.

Table A4. Eastern and Southern Africa: Current Account Exchange Restrictions, 1990 and 1999

	Article VIII Status		Date of Acceptance
	1990[1]	1999[1]	
Angola	no	no	
Botswana	no	yes	Nov. 1995
Burundi	no	no	
Comoros	no	yes	Jun. 1996
Congo, Dem. Rep. of	no	no	
Eritrea	no	no	
Ethiopia	no	no	
Kenya	no	yes	Jun. 1994
Lesotho	no	yes	Mar. 1997
Madagascar	no	yes	Sep. 1996
Malawi	no	yes	Dec. 1995
Mauritius	no	yes	Sep. 1993
Mozambique	no	no	
Namibia	no	yes	Sep. 1996
Rwanda	no	yes	Dec. 1998
Seychelles	yes	yes	Jan. 1978
South Africa	yes	yes	Sep. 1973
Swaziland	yes	yes	Dec. 1989
Tanzania	no	yes	Jul. 1996
Uganda	no	yes	Apr. 1994
Zambia	no	no	
Zimbabwe	no	yes	Feb. 1995
Total "yes"	3	15	
In percent of total	14	68	
Memorandum item			
IMF membership[2]	46	81	

Sources: IMF (1991); and IMF (2000).

[1]As of December 31.

[2]As of December 31, 1999, in percent of total.

Table A5. Eastern and Southern Africa: Nontariff Barriers to Imports, December 1998

	Quantitative Restrictions		Restrictive Licensing Requirements		Import State Trading Monopolies	Other[1]
	Bans	Quotas	For all products	For some products		
Angola	No	No	Yes	Yes	No	No
Botswana	No	Yes	No	Yes	No	No
Burundi	No	No	No	No	No	Yes
Comoros	No	No	No	No	Yes	No
Eritrea	Yes	No	No	Yes	Yes	No
Ethiopia	No	No	No	Yes	Yes	No
Kenya	No	No	No	No	No	No
Lesotho	No	No	No	No	No	No
Madagascar	No	No	No	No	No	No
Malawi	No	No	No	No	No	No
Mauritius	No	No	No	No	Yes	No
Mozambique	No	No	No	No	No	Yes
Namibia	No	Yes	No	Yes	Yes	No
Rwanda	No	No	No	No	No	No
Seychelles	No	Yes	Yes	…	Yes	No
South Africa	No	No	No	No	No	Yes
Swaziland	No	No	No	No	Yes	No
Tanzania	No	No	No	No	Yes	No
Uganda	Yes	No	No	No	No	No
Zambia	No	No	No	No	No	No
Zimbabwe	No	No	No	Yes	Yes	No

Sources: World Bank and IMF staff reports; and data provided by the authorities.

[1]Includes countervailing duties, dumping, etc.

Table A6. Eastern and Southern Africa: Nontariff Barriers to Exports, December 1998

	Quantitative Restrictions		Licensing[1]	Duties	Marketing Monopolies
	Bans	Quotas			
Angola	No	No	Yes	Yes	No
Botswana	No	No[2]	Yes[3]	No	Yes
Burundi	No	No	No	Yes	Yes
Comoros	No	No	No	Yes	No
Eritrea	Yes	No	No	No	No
Ethiopia	No	No	Yes	Yes	No
Kenya	No	No	Yes	No	Yes
Lesotho	No	No	No[2]	No	No
Madagascar	No	No	No	No	No
Malawi	No	No	No	No	No
Mauritius	No	No	No	No	No
Mozambique	No	No	No	Yes	No
Namibia	No	No[2]	Yes[3]	No	Yes
Rwanda	No	No	No	Yes	No
Seychelles	No	No	No	No	No
Swaziland	No	No	No	Yes	Yes
South Africa	No	No	No	Yes	No
Tanzania	No	No	No	No	No
Uganda	No	No	No	No	No
Zambia	Yes	No	No	No	No
Zimbabwe	No	Yes	Yes	No	Yes

Sources: World Bank and IMF staff reports; and data provided by the authorities.

[1]Only for restrictive (and not for statistical) purposes.

[2]Except for diamonds.

[3]All exports, except to SACU member countries, require a license. Within SACU, textiles and meat products require a license.

Table A7. Eastern and Southern Africa: Summary of Uruguay Round Commitments in Agriculture and Industry

	Agriculture					Industry						
	Average bound duty	Average bound ODC[1]	Total average tariff binding (duty+ODC)	Previous bindings	Share of lines bound in UR	Average bound duty	Average bound ODC	Total average binding (Duty+ODC)	Actual tariffs		Gap between bound and actual	
									(Early1990s)	(1998)	(Early 1990s)	(1998)
	(Percent)			(Percent of lines)		(Percent)						
Angola	80	0.1	80	0	4	80	0.1	80	24	24	56	56
Botswana	40	...	40	31	68	17	...	17	45	15	−28	2
Burundi	100	30	130	...	2	100	30	130	39	41	91	89
Kenya	100	0	100	0	2	54	0	54	44	19	10	35
Madagascar	30	250	280	...	11	30	250	280	30	18	250	262
Malawi	124	20	144	...	4	47	20	67	18	12	49	55
Mauritius	120	17	135	0	2	65	17	82	34	19	48	63
Mozambique	100	300	400	0	2	80	300	380	19	10	362	370
Namibia	40	0	40	31	68	17	0	17	45	15	−28	2
Rwanda	80	...	80	...	100	100	...	100	35	22	65	78
South Africa	40	...	40	17	98	17	...	17	45	15	−28	2
Swaziland	40	...	40	31	68	17	...	17	45	15	−28	2
Tanzania	120	120	240	0	0.1	120	120	240	25	20	215	220
Uganda	80	0	80	0	3	50	...	50	18	9	32	41
Zambia	124	0	124	...	4	42	...	42	37	14	5	28
Zimbabwe	146	15	161	8	1	38	29	66	30	32	36	34

Sources: Sorsa (1996); and IMF staff estimates.

[1]Other duties and charges.

Table A8. Eastern and Southern Africa: Commitments Undertaken in Trade in Services in the WTO

	Business	Communications	Construction	Distribution	Educational	Environmental	Financial	Health and Social	Tourism and Travel	Recreational	Transport	Other	Total
Angola	✓								✓	✓			3
Burundi	✓		✓				✓	✓	✓				5
Botswana		✓		✓					✓				3
Congo, Dem. Rep. of									✓	✓			2
Kenya	✓	✓	✓				✓		✓				5
Lesotho	✓	✓	✓	✓	✓		✓	✓	✓		✓	✓	10
Madagascar									✓				1
Malawi	✓		✓			✓	✓		✓				5
Mauritius		✓					✓		✓				3
Mozambique									✓				1
Namibia	✓											✓	2
Rwanda	✓	✓				✓	✓		✓				5
South Africa	✓		✓	✓	✓		✓	✓	✓	✓	✓		9
Swaziland						✓		✓	✓				3
Tanzania									✓				1
Uganda	✓	✓											2
Zambia	✓	✓					✓		✓				4
Zimbabwe									✓		✓	✓	3
Total	10	7	5	3	2	3	8	4	16	3	3	3	67

Source: Based on schedules of commitments submitted to the WTO.

Table A9. SADC: Intraregional and Extraregional Trade

	Imports			Exports		
	1990	1994	1999	1990	1994	1999
	(Millions of U.S. dollars)					
SADC trade						
Intraregional[1]	1,531	3,042	4,705	1,058	2,955	4,403
By SACU from/to rest of SADC region	79	560	571	402	2,004	3,135
By rest of SADC region from/to SACU	974	2,034	3,473	173	442	619
Between rest of SADC region	478	448	661	484	508	650
Extraregional	27,667	31,115	35,521	33,327	31,970	48,330
Rest of Africa	381	327	630	1,224	633	1,162
EU	12,502	13,393	15,665	9,277	7,656	14,880
United States	3,067	4,456	4,047	4,367	3,896	6,171
Japan	2,378	2,932	2,222	2,074	1,593	2,477
Rest of world	9,339	10,008	12,957	16,385	18,192	23,640
Total	29,199	34,158	40,226	34,386	34,924	52,733
	(Percent of total)					
SADC trade						
Intraregional	5.2	8.9	11.7	3.1	8.5	8.3
By SACU from/to rest of SADC region	0.3	1.6	1.4	1.2	5.7	5.9
By rest of SADC region from/to SACU	3.3	6.0	8.6	0.5	1.3	1.2
Between rest of SADC region	1.6	1.3	1.6	1.4	1.5	1.2
Extraregional	94.8	91.1	88.3	96.9	91.5	91.7
Rest of Africa	1.3	1.0	1.6	3.6	1.8	2.2
EU	42.8	39.2	38.9	27.0	21.9	28.2
United States	10.5	13.0	10.1	12.7	11.2	11.7
Japan	8.1	8.6	5.5	6.0	4.6	4.7
Rest of world	32.0	29.3	32.2	47.7	52.1	44.8
Total	100	100	100	100	100	100
	(Percent of GDP)					
Memorandum items						
Intraregional	0.9	1.7	2.6	0.6	1.7	2.5
Extraregional	16.9	17.6	19.9	20.4	18.0	27.0
Total	17.9	19.3	22.5	21.0	19.7	29.5

Source: IMF *Direction of Trade Statistics*.
[1]Import and export data differ mainly because partner country data are used directly or indirectly in estimating missing figures. Imports are measured c.i.f., exports are measured f.o.b.

Table A10. COMESA: Intraregional and Extraregional Trade

	Imports			Exports		
	1990	1994	1999	1990	1994	1999
	(Millions of U.S. dollars)					
COMESA trade						
Intraregional[1]	1,015	1,054	1,624	899	985	1,616
Extraregional	25,296	25,079	42,320	13,944	15,330	19,780
South Africa	982	1,854	3,932	169	428	696
Rest of Africa	388	315	291	320	495	205
EU	11,585	9,328	15,915	5,485	5,809	8,695
United States	2,302	2,663	4,259	2,939	3,231	3,923
Japan	1,305	1,270	1,845	588	592	711
Rest of world	8,733	9,649	16,077	4,443	4,774	5,550
Total	26,311	26,133	43,944	14,843	16,316	21,397
	(Percent of total)					
COMESA trade						
Intraregional	3.9	4.0	3.7	6.1	6.0	7.6
Extraregional	96.1	96.0	96.3	93.9	94.0	92.4
South Africa	3.7	7.1	8.9	1.1	2.6	3.3
Rest of Africa	1.5	1.2	0.7	2.2	3.0	1.0
EU	44.0	35.7	36.2	37.0	35.6	40.6
United States	8.8	10.2	9.7	19.8	19.8	18.3
Japan	5.0	4.9	4.2	4.0	3.6	3.3
Rest of world	33.2	36.9	36.6	29.9	29.3	25.9
Total	100	100	100	100	100	100
	(Percent of GDP)					
Memorandum items						
Intraregional	0.9	0.9	1.0	0.8	0.9	1.0
Extraregional	21.9	22.0	0.2	12.1	13.5	12.2
Total	22.8	22.9	1.2	12.8	14.3	13.2

Source: IMF, *Direction of Trade Statistics.*

[1]Import and export data differ mainly because partner country data are used directly or indirectly in estimating missing figures. Imports are measured c.i.f., exports are measured f.o.b.

Table A11. CBI: Intraregional and Extraregional Trade

	Imports			Exports		
	1990	1994	1999	1990	1994	1999
	(Millions of U.S. dollars)					
CBI trade						
Intraregional[1]	674	724	1,110	612	725	1,055
Extraregional	10,798	11,003	12,175	5,677	7,052	8,105
South Africa	984	1,670	2,867	169	320	594
Rest of Africa	329	134	126	364	485	399
EU	5,042	3,981	3,671	2,834	3,249	4,153
United States	634	584	531	521	621	722
Japan	743	705	565	362	368	417
Rest of world	3,066	3,930	4,415	1,425	2,009	1,820
Total	11,472	11,727	13,285	6,288	7,777	9,160
	(Percent of total)					
CBI trade						
Intraregional	5.9	6.2	8.4	9.7	9.3	11.5
Extraregional	94.1	93.8	91.6	90.3	90.7	88.5
South Africa	8.6	14.2	21.6	2.7	4.1	6.5
Rest of Africa	2.9	1.1	1.0	5.8	6.2	4.4
EU	43.9	33.9	27.6	45.1	41.8	45.3
United States	5.5	5.0	4.0	8.3	8.0	7.9
Japan	6.5	6.0	4.3	5.8	4.7	4.5
Rest of world	26.7	33.5	33.2	22.7	25.8	19.9
Total	100	100	100	100	100	100
	(Percent of GDP)					
Memorandum items						
Intraregional	1.5	1.9	2.2	1.4	1.9	2.1
Extraregional	24.5	28.5	0.3	12.9	18.3	16.1
Total	26.0	30.4	2.5	14.3	20.1	18.2

Source: IMF, *Direction of Trade Statistics*.

[1]Import and export data differ mainly because partner country data are used directly or indirectly in estimating missing figures. Imports are measured c.i.f., exports are measured f.o.b.

Table A12. Selected Eastern and Southern African Countries: Tariff Preferences
(In percent, unless otherwise indicated)

	OECD		European Union		Japan		USA		Export Loss if Preferences Eliminated		Export Loss under Uruguay Round
	Average tariff on exports	Average preference margin[1]	Average tariff on exports	Preference margin[1]	Average tariff on exports	Preference margin[1]	Average tariff on exports	Preference margin[1]	(Thousands of U.S. dollars)	(Percent of total exports)	(Percent of total exports)
Angola	0.2	1.5	0.3	3.2	1.8	0.0	0.1	0.4	3,497	0.3	...
Botswana	0.3	2.8	0.1	2.9	0.0	2.1	3.5	1.1	–399	–0.6	–0.3
Burundi	...	...	...	...	...	...	...	...	...	2.5	0.1
Comoros	...	...	...	...	...	...	...	...	...	0.6	0.1
Ethiopia	0.7	1.3	0.1	1.9	1.5	1.3	2.0	0.4	5,769	1.9	0.02
Lesotho	...	...	...	...	...	...	...	...	...	...	–3.4
Kenya	0.5	3.3	0.2	3.5	2.4	1.1	3.1	2.3	24,620	2.6	...
Madagascar	0.5	2.0	0.4	2.7	0.8	0.2	0.8	1.0	4,765	1.7	0.1
Malawi	1.1	2.4	0.1	3.5	0.0	0.1	5.4	0.6	2,776	1.4	0.1
Mozambique	...	...	...	...	...	...	...	...	...	1.3	0.1
Mauritius	1.3	3.1	0.2	3.4	4.8	1.1	6.4	1.8	47,441	4.8	...
Rwanda	...	...	...	...	...	...	...	...	...	3.8	0.1
Swaziland	0.8	4.4	0.5	4.9	6.7	3.0	3.5	1.9	2,939	1.7	...
Uganda	0.9	2.4	0.6	3.0	0.0	0.0	2.1	0.3	9,371	3.3	0.2
Tanzania	0.1	2.3	0.0	2.5	1.4	1.0	0.0	2.4	4,192	1.4	0.0
Zambia	0.3	1.7	0.5	2.9	0.0	0.6	1.4	1.4	7,297	1.0	0.5
Zimbabwe	0.9	2.5	0.2	3.3	1.2	1.0	4.0	1.0	19,770	1.4	...

Sources: Yeats (1994); and Harrold (1995).

[1] Difference between unweighted tariff faced by African exports and those paid by competitor countries.

Table A13. Sub-Saharan Africa: Compound Annual Growth Rates for Exports in U.S. Dollars
(Percent)

Exporting Country	1980–85	1985–90	1990–93	1993–96	1994–96
All non-oil goods					
Kenya	0.7	2.7	2.6	9.4	9.9
Madagascar	–8.5	3.4	5.4	18.9	12.4
Malawi	1.9	2.8	–0.4	5.5	1.4
Mauritius	–0.6	20.6	2.2	6.8	10.7
SACU	–6.9	7.2	–0.2	15.9	15.1
Uganda	–2.2	–10.4	–11.2	53.3	16.3
Zambia	–15.1	14.3	–13.5	–1.7	–7.3
Zimbabwe	11.0	12.1	–4.1	13.4	8.5
Eastern and Southern Africa (ESA) countries	–2.5	6.6	–2.4	15.2	8.4
ESA countries, excl. SACU	–1.8	6.5	–2.7	15.1	7.4
14 SSA countries	–5.2	6.5	0.0	14.4	12.4
All non-SSA countries	0.9	16.0	3.5	12.9	10.8
All foods					
Kenya	3.0	0.8	1.6	9.6	13.3
Madagascar	–9.0	0.5	5.3	11.5	4.0
Malawi	2.4	2.8	–0.5	6.2	1.3
Mauritius	–7.7	9.6	0.6	7.8	12.1
SACU	–12.8	11.8	–4.2	19.8	8.4
Uganda	–3.4	–10.7	–13.4	62.2	18.0
Zambia	–11.4	11.2	–2.6	14.4	34.0
Zimbabwe	10.9	14.1	1.0	14.3	4.0
ESA countries	–3.5	5.0	–1.5	18.2	11.9
ESA countries, excl. SACU	–2.2	4.0	–1.1	18.0	12.4
14 SSA countries	0.0	2.1	0.0	16.4	11.1
All non-SSA countries	–1.7	11.6	2.5	10.9	8.8
All manufactures					
Kenya	–6.9	10.9	5.7	1.6	–7.5
Madagascar	1.1	10.8	19.3	36.9	28.3
Malawi	–8.9	8.8	1.9	–10.6	–9.0
Mauritius	12.9	29.3	2.7	6.4	10.2
SACU[1]	–7.2	3.4	8.9	17.2	19.3
Uganda	–26.9	–8.1	30.8	–9.0	25.9
Zambia	–21.8	29.6	–1.8	7.3	8.8
Zimbabwe	3.2	14.1	–3.2	7.9	15.0
ESA countries	–6.8	12.4	8.0	7.2	11.4
ESA countries, excl. SACU	–6.8	13.6	7.9	5.8	10.2
14 SSA countries	–0.1	7.0	6.5	15.3	17.8
All non-SSA countries	2.2	17.0	4.1	13.2	11.4

Source: Yeats (1998).

Table A14. Sub-Saharan Africa: Structure of Exports, 1985–96

	Value (US$ million)	Percent Share in Total Exports					Manufactures Subgroup (Percent Share in Total Exports)						
		All foods	Agricultural materials	Fuels	Ores and metals	Manu-factures	Misc. goods	Leather and rubber	Wood and paper	Textiles	Iron and steel	Clothing	Footwear
Kenya													
1985	867	80.6	7.2	1.4	0.5	9.5	1.4	2.2	0.2	0.3	0.0	0.6	0.1
1990	992	73.0	9.7	1.4	1.3	13.7	1.4	5.1	0.3	0.4	0.0	0.6	0.1
1996	1,423	72.8	13.2	0.5	0.8	11.8	0.5	1.6	0.5	0.4	0.0	2.4	0.0
Madagascar													
1985	287	80.4	3.0	0.0	5.9	10.4	0.0	0.8	0.0	6.6	0.2	0.0	0.0
1990	331	71.1	5.0	0.4	8.1	14.9	0.4	1.1	0.1	5.9	0.0	3.4	0.0
1996	658	55.1	4.8	2.3	3.7	32.7	2.3	0.2	0.4	2.1	0.0	25.8	0.0
Malawi													
1985	263	93.7	2.6	0.0	0.0	3.4	0.0	0.0	0.0	3.0	0.0	0.1	0.0
1990	297	93.6	1.7	0.0	0.0	4.4	0.0	0.1	0.1	1.9	0.0	1.8	0.0
1996	343	95.3	1.5	0.0	0.1	3.0	0.0	0.0	0.1	1.1	0.0	1.0	0.0
Mauritius													
1985	475	51.5	0.8	0.0	0.1	47.5	0.0	0.1	0.2	1.5	0.2	36.9	0.0
1990	1,211	31.6	0.5	0.0	0.1	67.5	0.0	0.0	0.2	2.3	0.0	52.6	0.0
1996	1,581	31.7	0.5	0.0	0.0	67.3	0.0	0.0	0.1	2.2	0.0	54.6	0.1
South Africa													
1985	9,733	11.2	6.8	16.3	30.3	33.2	16.3	0.6	1.6	0.9	11.2	0.7	0.0
1990	13,154	14.3	6.1	12.6	36.6	29.0	12.8	0.8	2.0	0.7	8.9	0.7	0.0
1996	18,117	15.3	4.6	12.0	27.2	39.1	12.0	1.3	2.4	1.0	11.9	1.4	0.1
Uganda													
1985	404	87.9	11.0	0.0	0.1	0.9	0.0	0.0	0.0	0.0	0.0	0.0	0.0
1990	208	89.6	9.3	0.0	0.1	1.0	0.0	0.1	0.0	0.0	0.0	0.0	0.0
1996	564	95.5	3.6	0.0	0.0	0.6	0.0	0.2	0.0	0.0	0.0	0.0	0.0
Zambia													
1985	604	1.9	1.8	0.0	94.3	1.9	0.0	0.0	0.0	0.1	0.8	0.0	0.0
1990	1,087	1.6	0.7	0.0	93.8	3.8	0.0	0.1	0.0	0.9	0.0	0.1	0.0
1996	509	5.1	2.0	0.0	83.2	9.5	0.0	0.1	0.0	7.0	0.0	0.1	0.0
Zimbabwe													
1985	630	38.7	14.6	0.0	20.8	25.6	0.0	1.0	0.0	1.6	20.7	1.2	0.0
1990	1,035	40.6	9.4	0.0	22.1	27.7	0.0	0.9	0.0	2.0	18.7	3.3	0.0
1996	1,322	47.8	9.6	0.7	14.2	27.2	0.7	1.5	0.3	1.9	14.8	3.6	0.0
ESA countries													
1985	13,261	23.5	6.7	12.1	27.7	28.3	12.1	0.7	1.2	1.0	9.3	1.9	0.0
1990	18,313	22.5	5.7	9.1	33.3	28.2	9.2	0.9	1.5	1.0	7.4	4.3	0.0
1996	24,516	25.3	5.0	9.0	22.7	36.5	9.0	1.1	1.8	1.2	9.6	5.6	0.1
14 SSA countries													
1985	20,619	29.3	8.1	23.2	18.9	19.3	23.2	0.4	1.1	0.9	6.0	1.2	0.0
1990	26,103	25.2	9.3	18.4	25.0	21.3	18.4	0.7	1.5	0.9	5.2	3.1	0.0
1996	33,606	28.8	8.1	16.1	17.5	28.3	16.1	0.9	1.7	1.0	7.0	4.1	0.1

Source: Yeats (1998).

Table A15. Selected Eastern and Southern African Countries: Concentration of Exports, 1988 and 1996

| Exporter | Number of Items Exported[1] | | Share in Total Exports[2] (Percent) | | | |
| | | | 1988 | | 1996 | |
	1988	1996	Largest product	Three largest	Largest product	Three largest
Kenya	13	13	30	65	29	61
Madagascar	13	15	29	69	25	51
Malawi	8	6	62	84	74	90
Mauritius	11	9	50	87	55	84
South Africa	22	22	14	32	11	26
Uganda	5	6	90	95	80	92
Zambia	3	9	88	94	64	92
Zimbabwe	14	16	22	54	37	57

Source: Yeats (1998).

[1]Items are defined at the four-digit level of the Standard International Trade Classification (SITC) Revision 1 system. At this level, the SITC distinguishes among 632 individual products. To be included in the tabulation of an export product, the item had to account for 1 percent or more of total exports.

[2]The share of the largest and three largest four-digit SITC products in total exports.

Table A16. Selected Eastern and Southern African Countries: Intra-Industry Trade Ratios, 1988 and 1996

| Country | Year | Intra-Industry Trade Ratios[1] | | |
		Transport and machinery	Other manufactures	All manufactures
Kenya	1988	0.04	0.10	0.07
	1996	0.05	0.14	0.11
Madagascar	1988	0.01	0.06	0.04
	1996	0.02	0.12	0.09
Malawi	1988	0.02	0.05	0.04
	1996	0.03	0.11	0.08
Mauritius	1988	0.04	0.20	0.15
	1996	0.09	0.18	0.15
South Africa	1988	0.07	0.25	0.18
	1996	0.20	0.36	0.30
Uganda	1988	0.02	0.02	0.02
	1996	0.02	0.02	0.02
Zambia	1988	0.02	0.05	0.04
	1996	0.01	0.04	0.03
Zimbabwe	1988	0.02	0.07	0.06
	1996	0.02	0.13	0.10
Memorandum items				
Brazil	1996	0.57	0.50	0.53
Chile	1996	0.08	0.28	0.22
Rep. of Korea	1996	0.56	0.56	0.55
Turkey	1996	0.23	0.34	0.28
Taiwan, Province of China	1996	0.64	0.52	0.57

Source: Yeats (1998).

[1]The intra-industry trade ratio for any industry i is calculated as $I_i = 1 - (|X_i - M_i|) / (X_i + M_i)$, where X_i and M_i are the industry's exports and imports, respectively. The value of the index lies between 0 (no intra-industry trade) and 1 (full intra-industry trade).

Table A17. Eastern and Southern Africa: Economic Conditions, 1990–92
(Average annual rate in percent, unless otherwise indicated)

	GDP Growth	GDP Per Capita Growth	Export Volume Growth	Inflation	Investment-to-GDP Ratio (Percent)	Fiscal Balance, Excluding Grants (Percent of GDP)	Current Account Balance, Excluding Grants (Percent of GDP)
Moderate or no liberalization							
Angola	−1.8	−4.5	4.3	128.5	4.7	−17.2	−8.0
Burundi	3.1	0.1	11.0	6.8	14.6	−10.4	−19.6
Comoros	2.7	1.9	7.2	−2.4	20.7	−17.2	−19.5
Ethiopia	−2.5	−5.5	−24.8	15.7	10.4	−11.1	−4.4
Kenya	1.8	−1.1	2.1	19.4	20.9	−8.3	−5.2
Madagascar	−0.7	−4.0	2.0	11.9	5.1	−7.6	−11.5
Mauritius	5.3	4.2	0.9	8.8	30.0	−2.3	−2.8
Rwanda	0.9	−1.9	4.6	11.1	12.3	−11.8	−10.4
Seychelles	5.7	4.9	13.1	3.1	22.6	−5.1	−6.2
Tanzania	3.2	0.6	−0.3	26.8	26.6	−5.3	−16.9
Zimbabwe	1.2	−1.9	−5.9	27.6	18.9	−7.4	−7.2
Average	1.7	−0.6	1.3	23.4	17.0	−9.4	−10.2
Substantial liberalization							
Botswana	5.9	3.1	3.5	13.1	21.3	8.5	1.6
Lesotho	4.7	1.1	26.1	15.5	8.9	−8.4	−57.4
Malawi	2.4	−0.9	11.8	14.4	8.2	−8.4	−12.9
Namibia	3.3	−0.1	2.9	13.9	24.9	−3.7	−11.7
South Africa	−1.2	−3.9	3.1	14.5	16.2	−5.5	1.1
Swaziland	4.5	1.0	3.8	10.9	22.2	2.6	−10.1
Mozambique	−0.7	−2.6	10.8	40.7	15.7	−16.1	−32.8
Uganda	3.5	0.7	18.2	36.2	17.4	−11.1	−15.9
Zambia	0.3	−3.3	−0.6	124.3	13.4	−13.8	−16.1
Average	2.5	−0.5	8.9	31.5	16.5	−6.2	−17.1

Sources: IMF, African Department database, and World Economic Outlook database.

Table A18. Eastern and Southern Africa: Economic Conditions
(Average annual rate between 1993 and 1999, unless otherwise indicated)

	GDP Growth	GDP Per Capita Growth	Export Volume Growth	Inflation	Investment-to-GDP Ratio (Percent)	Fiscal Balance, Excluding Grants (Percent of GDP)	Current Account Balance, Excluding Grants (Percent of GDP)	Average Annual Real Exchange Rate Depreciation (1990–98)
Moderate or no liberalization								
Angola	2.0	–0.8	7.4	1,373.5	14.0	–17.6	–21.6	–8.8
Burundi	–2.2	–3.1	4.4	17.4	10.6	–8.5	–12.2	–1.3
Comoros	–0.8	–3.4	–4.4	5.8	21.7	–14.3	–19.1	—
Ethiopia	6.3	3.2	11.7	3.8	17.2	–7.8	–8.1	6.0
Kenya	2.5	–0.3	5.6	15.2	19.0	–2.8	–3.0	–3.9
Madagascar	2.6	–0.5	9.6	19.6	12.1	–8.7	–9.4	0.1
Mauritius	5.2	3.9	1.8	7.0	27.9	–4.1	–0.7	–0.1
Rwanda	2.6	3.2	–0.3	17.6	11.0	–11.4	–22.2	–1.6
Seychelles	2.6	0.7	24.7	0.7	34.3	–11.5	–11.1	0.1
Tanzania	3.3	0.5	4.4	20.7	19.1	–4.3	–17.9	–5.1
Zimbabwe	3.3	0.0	2.7	29.3	21.7	–9.3	–4.4	9.6
Average	2.5	0.3	6.2	137.3	18.9	–9.1	–11.8	–1.3
Substantial liberalization								
Botswana	5.1	2.5	6.9	9.8	28.4	2.0	5.0	–0.9
Lesotho	3.4	1.1	8.6	8.9	49.0	–3.8	–48.2	0.6
Malawi	5.5	2.3	5.9	37.5	16.4	–13.9	–15.3	2.7
Namibia	2.6	–0.4	–0.1	8.2	20.4	–4.4	–7.9	0.3
South Africa	2.3	0.0	4.6	7.9	16.3	–4.8	–0.2	1.5
Swaziland	2.3	0.0	4.6	7.9	16.3	–4.8	–0.2	0.2
Mozambique	8.7	6.3	11.8	30.4	20.7	–13.3	–28.7	2.7
Uganda	7.1	4.1	17.5	9.1	17.7	–7.4	–8.5	1.3
Zambia	–0.9	–2.9	–2.1	55.9	14.0	–10.4	–13.1	–1.3
Average	4.0	1.4	6.4	19.5	22.1	–6.7	–13.0	0.7

Sources: IMF, African Deparment database, and World Economic Outlook database.

References

Amjadi, Ayita, Ulrich Reinke, and Alexander J. Yeats, 1996, "Did External Barriers Cause the Marginalization of Sub-Saharan Africa in World Trade?", World Bank Discussion Paper No. 348 (Washington: World Bank).

Amjadi, Ayita, and Alexander J. Yeats, 1995, "Have Transport Costs Contributed to the Relative Decline of African Exports? Some Preliminary Empirical Evidence," World Bank Policy Research Working Paper No. 1559 (Washington: World Bank).

Collier, Paul, and Jan Willem Gunning, 1999, "Explaining African Economic Performance," *Journal of Economic Literature*, Vol. 37 (March), pp. 64–111.

Dollar, David, 1992, "Outward-Oriented Developing Economies Really Do Grow More Rapidly: Evidence from 95 LDCs, 1976–1985," *Economic Development and Cultural Change*, Vol. 40 (April), pp. 523–44.

Easterly, William, and Ross Levine, 1997, "Africa's Growth Tragedy: Policies and Ethnic Divisions," *Quarterly Journal of Economics*, Vol. 112 (November), pp. 1203–50.

Ebrill, Liam P., Janet Stotsky, and Renit Gropp, 1999, *Revenue Implications of Trade Liberalization*, IMF Occasional Paper No. 180 (Washington: International Monetary Fund).

Edwards, Sebastian, 1998, "Openness, Productivity and Growth: What Do We Really Know?", *Economic Journal*, Vol. 108 (March), pp. 383–98.

Gelbard, Enrique, and Sérgio Pereira Leite, 1999, "Measuring Financial Development in Sub-Saharan Africa," IMF Working Paper 99/105 (Washington: International Monetary Fund).

Harrold, Peter, 1995, "The Impact of the Uruguay Round on Africa," World Bank Discussion Paper No. 311 (Washington: World Bank).

IDS (Institute of Development Studies), and BIDPA (Botswana Institute for Development Policy Analysis), 1998, "Study to Assess the Economic Impact of the Proposed European Union–South Africa Free Trade Agreement on Botswana, Lesotho, Namibia, and Swaziland," Final Report, December.

IMANI, 1997, "Impact of the EU-SA Free Trade Agreement on BLNS Countries," Consultants' Report.

IMF, 1991, *Exchange Arrangements and Exchange Restrictions: Annual Report 1991* (Washington: International Monetary Fund).

———, 2000, *Exchange Arrangements and Exchange Restrictions: Annual Report 2000* (forthcoming, Washington: International Monetary Fund).

ITU, 1999, *International Telecommunication Union Report* (Geneva: International Telecommunication Union).

Jonsson, Gunnar, and Arvind Subramanian, 2000, "Dynamic Gains from Trade: Evidence from South Africa," IMF Working Paper (forthcoming; Washington: International Monetary Fund).

Madani, Dorsati, 1999, "A Review of the Role and Impact of Export Processing Zones," World Bank Policy Research Working Paper No. 2238 (Washington: World Bank).

Mattoo, Aaditya, 1999, "Financial Services and the World Trade Organization: Liberalization Commitments of the Developing and Transition Economies," World Bank Policy Research Working Paper No. 2184 (Washington: World Bank).

Mattoo, Aaditya, Randeep Rathindran, and Arvind Subramanian, 2000, "Measuring Liberalization in Services and Its Impact on Growth," mimeo (Washington: World Bank).

Rodrik, Dani, 1998, "Why Is Trade Reform So Difficult in Africa?", *Journal of African Economies*, Vol. 7, Supplement 1 (June), pp. 43–69.

———, 1999, *The New Global Economy and Developing Countries: Making Openness Work* (Baltimore, Maryland: Johns Hopkins University Press for the Overseas Development Council).

Sachs, Jeffrey D., and Andrew Warner, 1995, "Economic Reform and the Process of Global Integration," *Brookings Papers on Economic Activity: 1,* Brookings Institution, pp. 1–118.

———, 1997, "Fundamental Sources of Long-Run Growth," *American Economic Review, Papers and Proceedings*, Vol. 87 (May), pp. 184–88.

Sharer, Robert, and others, 1998, *Trade Liberalization in IMF-Supported Programs*, World Economic and Financial Surveys (Washington: International Monetary Fund).

Sorsa, Piritta, 1996, "Sub-Saharan African Own Commitments in the Uruguay Round: Myth or Reality?", *World Economy*, Vol. 19 (May), pp. 287–305.

Subramanian, Arvind, and Natalia Tamirisa, "Africa's Trade Revisited," forthcoming (Washington: International Monetary Fund).

Wang, Zhen Kun, and L. Alan Winters, 1998, "Africa's Role in Multilateral Trade Negotiations: Past and Future," *Journal of African Economies*, Vol. 7, Supplement 1 (June), pp. 1–33.

World Bank, *World Development Indicators*, 1999 (Washington: World Bank).

Yeats, Alexander J., 1994, "What Are OECD Trade Preferences Worth to Sub-Saharan Africa?", World Bank Policy Research Working Paper No. 1254 (Washington: World Bank).

———, 1998, "What Can Be Expected from African Regional Trade Arrangements? Some Empirical Evidence," World Bank Policy Research Working Paper No. 2004 (Washington: World Bank).

———, and Francis Ng, 1999, "Good Governance and Trade Policy: Are They the Keys to Africa's Global Integration and Growth?", World Bank Policy Research Working Paper No. 2038 (Washington: World Bank).

Recent Occasional Papers of the International Monetary Fund

196. Trade and Trade Policies in Eastern and Southern Africa, by a staff team led by Arvind Subramanian, with Enrique Gelbard, Richard Harmsen, Katrin Elborgh-Woytek, and Piroska Nagy. 2000.

195. The Eastern Caribbean Currency Union—Institutions, Performance, and Policy Issues, by Frits van Beek, José Roberto Rosales, Mayra Zermeño, Ruby Randall, and Jorge Shepherd. 2000.

194. Fiscal and Macroeconomic Impact of Privatization, by Jeffrey Davis, Rolando Ossowski, Thomas Richardson, and Steven Barnett. 2000.

193. Exchange Rate Regimes in an Increasingly Integrated World Economy, by Michael Mussa, Paul Masson, Alexander Swoboda, Esteban Jadresic, Paolo Mauro, and Andy Berg. 2000.

192. Macroprudential Indicators of Financial System Soundness, by a staff team led by Owen Evans, Alfredo M. Leone, Mahinder Gill, and Paul Hilbers. 2000.

191. Social Issues in IMF-Supported Programs, by Sanjeev Gupta, Louis Dicks-Mireaux, Ritha Khemani, Calvin McDonald, and Marijn Verhoeven. 2000.

190. Capital Controls: Country Experiences with Their Use and Liberalization, by Akira Ariyoshi, Karl Habermeier, Bernard Laurens, Inci Ötker-Robe, Jorge Iván Canales Kriljenko, and Andrei Kirilenko. 2000.

189. Current Account and External Sustainability in the Baltics, Russia, and Other Countries of the Former Soviet Union, by Donal McGettigan. 2000.

188. Financial Sector Crisis and Restructuring: Lessons from Asia, by Carl-Johan Lindgren, Tomás J.T. Baliño, Charles Enoch, Anne-Marie Gulde, Marc Quintyn, and Leslie Teo. 1999.

187. Philippines: Toward Sustainable and Rapid Growth, Recent Developments and the Agenda Ahead, by Markus Rodlauer, Prakash Loungani, Vivek Arora, Charalambos Christofides, Enrique G. De la Piedra, Piyabha Kongsamut, Kristina Kostial, Victoria Summers, and Athanasios Vamvakidis. 2000.

186. Anticipating Balance of Payments Crises: The Role of Early Warning Systems, by Andrew Berg, Eduardo Borensztein, Gian Maria Milesi-Ferretti, and Catherine Pattillo. 1999.

185. Oman Beyond the Oil Horizon: Policies Toward Sustainable Growth, edited by Ahsan Mansur and Volker Treichel. 1999.

184. Growth Experience in Transition Countries, 1990–98, by Oleh Havrylyshyn, Thomas Wolf, Julian Berengaut, Marta Castello-Branco, Ron van Rooden, and Valerie Mercer-Blackman. 1999.

183. Economic Reforms in Kazakhstan, Kyrgyz Republic, Tajikistan, Turkmenistan, and Uzbekistan, by Emine Gürgen, Harry Snoek, Jon Craig, Jimmy McHugh, Ivailo Izvorski, and Ron van Rooden. 1999.

182. Tax Reform in the Baltics, Russia, and Other Countries of the Former Soviet Union, by a Staff Team Led by Liam Ebrill and Oleh Havrylyshyn. 1999.

181. The Netherlands: Transforming a Market Economy, by C. Maxwell Watson, Bas B. Bakker, Jan Kees Martijn, and Ioannis Halikias. 1999.

180. Revenue Implications of Trade Liberalization, by Liam Ebrill, Janet Stotsky, and Reint Gropp. 1999.

179. Dinsinflation in Transition: 1993–97, by Carlo Cottarelli and Peter Doyle. 1999.

178. IMF-Supported Programs in Indonesia, Korea, and Thailand: A Preliminary Assessment, by Timothy Lane, Atish Ghosh, Javier Hamann, Steven Phillips, Marianne Schulze-Ghattas, and Tsidi Tsikata. 1999.

177. Perspectives on Regional Unemployment in Europe, by Paolo Mauro, Eswar Prasad, and Antonio Spilimbergo. 1999.

176. Back to the Future: Postwar Reconstruction and Stabilization in Lebanon, edited by Sena Eken and Thomas Helbling. 1999.

175. Macroeconomic Developments in the Baltics, Russia, and Other Countries of the Former Soviet Union, 1992–97, by Luis M. Valdivieso. 1998.

174. Impact of EMU on Selected Non–European Union Countries, by R. Feldman, K. Nashashibi, R. Nord, P. Allum, D. Desruelle, K. Enders, R. Kahn, and H. Temprano-Arroyo. 1998.

173. The Baltic Countries: From Economic Stabilization to EU Accession, by Julian Berengaut, Augusto Lopez-Claros, Françoise Le Gall, Dennis Jones, Richard Stern, Ann-Margret Westin, Effie Psalida, Pietro Garibaldi. 1998.

172. Capital Account Liberalization: Theoretical and Practical Aspects, by a staff team led by Barry Eichengreen and Michael Mussa, with Giovanni Dell'Ariccia, Enrica Detragiache, Gian Maria Milesi-Ferretti, and Andrew Tweedie. 1998.

171. Monetary Policy in Dollarized Economies, by Tomás Baliño, Adam Bennett, and Eduardo Borensztein. 1998.

170. The West African Economic and Monetary Union: Recent Developments and Policy Issues, by a staff team led by Ernesto Hernández-Catá and comprising Christian A. François, Paul Masson, Pascal Bouvier, Patrick Peroz, Dominique Desruelle, and Athanasios Vamvakidis. 1998.

169. Financial Sector Development in Sub-Saharan African Countries, by Hassanali Mehran, Piero Ugolini, Jean Phillipe Briffaux, George Iden, Tonny Lybek, Stephen Swaray, and Peter Hayward. 1998.

168. Exit Strategies: Policy Options for Countries Seeking Greater Exchange Rate Flexibility, by a staff team led by Barry Eichengreen and Paul Masson with Hugh Bredenkamp, Barry Johnston, Javier Hamann, Esteban Jadresic, and Inci Ötker. 1998.

167. Exchange Rate Assessment: Extensions of the Macroeconomic Balance Approach, edited by Peter Isard and Hamid Faruqee. 1998

166. Hedge Funds and Financial Market Dynamics, by a staff team led by Barry Eichengreen and Donald Mathieson with Bankim Chadha, Anne Jansen, Laura Kodres, and Sunil Sharma. 1998.

165. Algeria: Stabilization and Transition to the Market, by Karim Nashashibi, Patricia Alonso-Gamo, Stefania Bazzoni, Alain Féler, Nicole Laframboise, and Sebastian Paris Horvitz. 1998.

164. MULTIMOD Mark III: The Core Dynamic and Steady-State Model, by Douglas Laxton, Peter Isard, Hamid Faruqee, Eswar Prasad, and Bart Turtelboom. 1998.

163. Egypt: Beyond Stabilization, Toward a Dynamic Market Economy, by a staff team led by Howard Handy. 1998.

162. Fiscal Policy Rules, by George Kopits and Steven Symansky. 1998.

161. The Nordic Banking Crises: Pitfalls in Financial Liberalization? by Burkhard Dress and Ceyla Pazarbaşıoğlu. 1998.

160. Fiscal Reform in Low-Income Countries: Experience Under IMF-Supported Programs, by a staff team led by George T. Abed and comprising Liam Ebrill, Sanjeev Gupta, Benedict Clements, Ronald McMorran, Anthony Pellechio, Jerald Schiff, and Marijn Verhoeven. 1998.

159. Hungary: Economic Policies for Sustainable Growth, Carlo Cottarelli, Thomas Krueger, Reza Moghadam, Perry Perone, Edgardo Ruggiero, and Rachel van Elkan. 1998.

158. Transparency in Government Operations, by George Kopits and Jon Craig. 1998.

157. Central Bank Reforms in the Baltics, Russia, and the Other Countries of the Former Soviet Union, by a staff team led by Malcolm Knight and comprising Susana Almuiña, John Dalton, Inci Otker, Ceyla Pazarbaşıoğlu, Arne B. Petersen, Peter Quirk, Nicholas M. Roberts, Gabriel Sensenbrenner, and Jan Willem van der Vossen. 1997.

156. The ESAF at Ten Years: Economic Adjustment and Reform in Low-Income Countries, by the staff of the International Monetary Fund. 1997.

155. Fiscal Policy Issues During the Transition in Russia, by Augusto Lopez-Claros and Sergei V. Alexashenko. 1998.

154. Credibility Without Rules? Monetary Frameworks in the Post–Bretton Woods Era, by Carlo Cottarelli and Curzio Giannini. 1997.

153. Pension Regimes and Saving, by G.A. Mackenzie, Philip Gerson, and Alfredo Cuevas. 1997.

152. Hong Kong, China: Growth, Structural Change, and Economic Stability During the Transition, by John Dodsworth and Dubravko Mihaljek. 1997.

Note: For information on the title and availability of Occasional Papers not listed, please consult the IMF Publications Catalog or contact IMF Publication Services.